The Texas Country Music Hall of Fame

By Bill O'Neal
and
Tommie Ritter Smith

With an Introduction by Duane Allen

EAKIN PRESS ✦ Fort Worth, Texas
www.EakinPress.com

Copyright © 2022
By Bill O'Neal & Tommie Ritter Smith
Published By Eakin Press
An Imprint of Wild Horse Media Group
P.O. Box 331779
Fort Worth, Texas 76163
1-817-344-7036
www.EakinPress.com
ALL RIGHTS RESERVED
1 2 3 4 5 6 7 8 9
Paperback ISBN 978-1-68179-263-7
Hardback ISBN 978-1-68179-345-0
eBook ISBN 978-1-68179-346-7

Dedicated to Bill Smith

Beloved husband of Tommie Ritter Smith
Longtime friend of Bill O'Neal

Bill Smith was part of the Texas Music Tradition. A superb bass, he performed and recorded gospel music with the Calvary Boys for 40 years.

Bill volunteered whenever needed at the Texas Country Music Hall of Fame. On numerous occasions he donned one of Tex Ritter's Western suits and sang the star's hits for busloads of tourists or museum events.

Contents

Acknowledgments

Both of us have enjoyed country music throughout our lives. However, Tommie vastly expanded her country music horizons during her decades-long efforts to create and maintain the Texas Country Music Hall of Fame. From Willie Nelson to Mickey Gilley, from Gene Autry to Jeannie C. Riley, Tommie has acquired a vast number of friends and contacts throughout the country music industry. From these connections, she has accumulated a wealth of anecdotes and personal details which enliven our history of the Texas Country Music Hall of Fame. And during each annual Hall of Fame induction weekend, hundreds of never-before-published images were taken by TCMHOF photographers, from which we have illustrated this book.

Bill's youthful enjoyment of country and southern gospel music was explained and interpreted during graduate work at the University of Texas by Dr. Bill Malone, author of the authoritative *Country Music USA*. Bill O'Neal subsequently expanded his lecture on "Texas Musical Traditions," delivering it for more than thirty years to his Texas history students at Panola College while using it for programs and inserts in books.

Charles Thomas, longtime city manager of Carthage, was an indispensable force behind the financing and construction of the Texas Country Music Hall of Fame building. Charles and his wife now live in Longview, and when Bill requested an interview, he was invited to lunch. Both Charles and Linda provided depth and detail regarding the crucial periods of construction and expansion, and I am deeply grateful for their hospitality.

Tommie persuaded Duane Allen to provide an introduction to this book, which we greatly appreciate. We are thankful, too, for the generosity of country artists and their families for donating or loaning the TCMHOF artifacts and memorabilia, without which our museum would not exist. Their eagerness to share prized family possessions through the Texas Country Music Hall of Fame continues to bless the museum and our patrons.

Dr. Berri O'Neal expertly converted a handwritten manuscript to electronic form, created a large photo file, and utilized her photography skills on our behalf. She has proven her capabilities on several of Bill's previous projects, and the authors deeply appreciate her efforts with this book.

Of course, our deepest gratitude is owed to the countless country music performers and songwriters who created the artistic sounds we honor at the Texas Country Music Hall of Fame.

Tommie Ritter Smith
Bill O'Neal

Foreword

By Duane Allen
The Oak Ridge Boys

The first time I walked into the Texas Country Music Hall of Fame I knew I was home.

It wasn't beautiful because of the beautiful architecture — and it is beautiful — with its soaring ceilings and welcoming entryway. And it wasn't because of the $2.5 million state-of-the-art museum, which houses treasured artifacts of Texas-born entertainers — from the early singing cowboys to modern day disc jockeys. It wasn't because of the Hall of Fame's location in East Texas. The city of Carthage is more than an hour away from my hometown of Taylortown.

It was because of the people.

When I first stepped inside the doors of the Texas Country Music Hall of Fame, it was a hot August morning. But I was chilled to the bone by the seeming omnipresence of all of those who had entered - or been honored there posthumously – before me. Tex Ritter. Jim Reeves. Gene Autry. Bob Wills. Ray Price. Jimmy Dean. They had all had an early influence on my personal musical dreams and ambitions.

On that ninth day of August in 2014, I also had no way of knowing that others would soon join that list. Many of whom I have called close, personal friends and colleagues throughout the years. People like Kenny Rogers, The Chuck Wagon Gang, and Rodney Crowell.

However, when you talk about the people of the Texas Country Music Hall of Fame, you must begin your conversation with the name Tommie Ritter Smith. Tommie, who was at one time the Director of the Panola County Chamber of Commerce in Carthage, had big dreams too. Her dream was to establish the Texas Country Music Hall of Fame. And her vision was pieced together slowly out of love, dedication, and hard work.

In 1993, Tommie established the Tex Ritter Museum. A few years later, she expanded it to include other Texas-born country music legends. And, in 1998, the Hall of Fame opened its doors.

Four years later, in 2002, the permanent building for the Hall of Fame was dedicated. And two years after that, in August 2004, the museum and event center were expanded to include a significant Jim Reeves exhibit – just one of the main displays that would eventually become a part of the multi-million-dollar facility.

The Texas Country Music Hall of Fame is, indeed, a beautiful edifice. A state-of-the-art museum and events center. But it would be just an empty building without the people behind it. People you will meet inside this book.

Come on in. Take a seat. And enjoy the story as it unfolds.

Chapter One
Welcome to the Texas Country Music Hall of Fame

"Wow!"

Marty Stuart, a dynamic performer who was in Carthage as a guest artist for the 2005 Hall of Fame induction, was guided into the museum by Tommie Ritter Smith, president, and founder of the Texas Country Music Hall of Fame (TCM-HOF).

Entering the large display area for the first time, Stuart clearly was overwhelmed by the colorful and historic displays arrayed before him. He looked intently at one exhibit case after another. Tommie Ritter Smith felt reluctant to interrupt the country music star's intense concentration, and a couple of long, silent moments passed before Stuart finally exclaimed, "Wow!"

Marty Stuart is a member of the *Grand Ole Opry* and Nashville's Country Music Hall of Fame, and he has won five Grammy Awards. But this stellar performer was impressed to

When Marty Stuart was ushered into the museum of the Texas Country Music Hall of Fame by Tommie Ritter Smith, the gifted star gazed in wonder before exclaiming, "Wow!"

the point of hushed contemplation as he first viewed the Hall of Fame devoted to Texas country music artists. Similar reactions have swept over thousands of other country music fans and performers when they first visited this shrine to the galaxy of distinguished Lone Star musicians located — fittingly — in a small country town amid the piney woods of East Texas.

* * * *

The TCMHOF stands two blocks from the Carthage town square. A long, low wall in front of the brick and glass building announces, in bright blue letters: "Texas Country Music Hall of Fame and the Tex Ritter Museum." A larger-than-life bronze statue of Tex Ritter, strumming a guitar beside his horse White Flash, dominates the approach to the entrance, along with a set of tall flagpoles flying the Lone Star banner.

Passing through the glass doors, visitors look up at images stretching to the ceiling and focus on local superstars Tex Ritter and "Gentleman" Jim Reeves. Entry into the museum is through the gift shop, which offers country music recordings, photos of the stars, glittering country music "record" purses, vests, and jackets in denim, black and white. There are necklaces and bracelets, hats and caps, t-shirts with bling and country monograms, and books about such stars as Tex Ritter, Willie Nelson, and Gene Autry. A children's section offers coloring books, country toys, and cowboy Christmas items. The gift shop offers a cornucopia of country music souvenirs.

An entrance from the gift shop leads to a spacious event room. There is a small performance stage, and lecture-hall seating can accommodate an audience of 300. For dining events, more than

200 guests may sit around tables.

From this banquet room or through another entrance from the gift shop, patrons may enter the exhibit hall — the big display area that elicited a "Wow!" from Marty Stuart.

An eye-catching movie marquee introduces visitors to a small version of a 1930s motion picture theater. There are five rows of wooden seats taken from an old movie house in East Texas. Colorful movie posters are everywhere, including *Tex Ritter and the Boy Scouts*, *Deep in the Heart of Texas* (starring Tex Ritter, of course), and another of Ritter's sixty films, *Arizona Frontier* (co-starring legendary athlete Jim Thorpe). A different poster publicizes *Oh Susannah!*, a Gene Autry horse opera. Two other posters advertise *Problem Child* and *Hero at Large*, both of which feature John Ritter. Around this little theater are movie stills and the history of Tex Ritter's movie career.

Nearby stands a jukebox. There is booth seating, and museum visitors may sit and play one country music favorite after another — free of charge. The jukebox exerted a profound effect upon American popular music, with a powerful influence on country western during the 1930s, 1940s, and 1950s.

Near the jukebox is an extensive Jim Reeves collection, featuring a replica of the KGRI radio studio in nearby Henderson where Reeves first worked in the field of music. A mannequin of deejay Reeves stands at the microphone, surrounded by studio equipment of the late 1940s. Outside the big window of the studio are display cases with memorabilia celebrating the brilliant career of Gentleman Jim. Among the exhibits are performance costumes and a guitar, along with a vintage baseball glove and a St. Louis Cardinals uniform, representing Jim's injury-shortened career as a pitcher in the Cardinal minor league

The Texas Country Music Hall of Fame building opened in 2002.

The statue of Tex Ritter and White Flash is the most photographed object at the TCMHOF.

system.

Throughout the museum display cases abound, including at least one for each inductee. Virtually every artist donated colorful costumes. Western suits are everywhere, many of them created by the well-known Nudie the Tailor (his coveted labels read "Nudie's RODEO TAILORS, North Hollywood, California"). There are gaudy Western shirts, fringed Western dresses, Western boots and hats.

Michael Martin Murphey provided a pair of high-topped boots, colored in green and white and featuring shamrocks — as befits an Irish cowboy named Murphey. Tracy Byrd contributed a pair of big black boots with "Dallas Cowboys" on the tops, including the famous logo star of the team. Johnny Rodriguez donated a striking Tejano shirt. The celebrated country music deejay and songwriter Bill Mack gave the

museum a denim jacket bearing his famous nickname, "The Midnight Cowboy." Mickey Gilley's display not only showcases costumes —there also is a unique beer can labeled: "Gilley's — A Premium Texas Beer."

Bobbie Nelson, sister of Willie and an enormously gifted pianist, presented the museum with a black performance outfit featuring a white piano keyboard. Charter inductee Cindy Walker was given a white evening gown by her mother, who extracted a promise that Cindy would wear it when she entered Nashville's Country Music Hall of Fame. Cindy promised, and she wore it in 1997 when she was inducted. She wore the gown again the following year upon her induction to the Texas Country Music Hall of Fame. Cindy attended each TCMHOF induction for the rest of her life, and she happily wore the gown on each occasion in memory of her mother.

The museum collection included several saddles, including one used by Bob Wills and three ridden by Tex Ritter aboard White Flash during Western movies and personal appearance tours. As crucial as saddles are to cowboys, a Nikon F camera with a fifty mm lens was to Les Leverett, who served for thirty-two years as a staff photographer for the *Grand Ole Opry*. Les shot thousands upon thousands of photos of Country Music stars and *Grand Ole Opry* performances with this historic camera, which now resides in the TCMHOF Museum.

In addition to performance costumes, Charlie Walker donated his post-World War II U.S. Army uniform, complete with his military medals. Dorothy Fay Ritter, a beautiful movie starlet who married Tex in 1941, gave up her film career to be a wife and mother. But during World War II, she toured military bases with Tex, and later Dorothy Fay went on a six-month tour of overseas bases in the Central Pacific with the Special Services of the U.S. Armed Forces. Dorothy and her fellow female troupers usually wore fatigues, but she also was issued a dress uniform.

Both the dress uniform and a set of her fatigues are on display in the movie theater space.

Gene Autry was an experienced pilot of small planes, and six months after Pearl Harbor, he put his lucrative career on hold and volunteered for the U.S Army Air Corps. Sergeant Autry flew a C-109 transport plane in the Air Transport Command in the Pacific Theater and was periodically assigned to Special Services duty. He served for the duration of the war. In the museum, he is pictured in uniform next to the uniforms of Dorothy Fay Ritter. And on the evening before his induction into the TCMHOF in 2003, former Army Captain Kris Kristofferson and his wife Lisa worked until past midnight arranging his Ranger uniform carefully and precisely in its museum case.

Not all uniforms in the museum are military. Linda Davis, a 2009 inductee and a graduate of Carthage schools, has provided the museum with her CHS cheerleader letter jacket and her big cheerleader megaphone. This display faces the case with the Cardinal baseball uniform of Jim Reeves and not far away is the summer

The entrance to the TCMHOF features Tex Ritter and Gentleman Jim Reeves, two natives of Panola County who each were voted into Nashville's Country Music Hall of Fame.

The Texas Country Music Hall of Fame gift shop.

league baseball jersey of John Ritter.

Near the center of the museum is a striking display reminding visitors that a great many Lone Star artists reached the pinnacle of country music success by performing as members of the *Grand Ole Opry*. A bright mockup of the famous Opry stage ("WSM Nashville — Grand Ole Opry" reads the historic sign) has room for costumed mannequins of six Texas superstars. Tex Ritter and Gentleman Jim Reeves stand in front, while slightly behind these Panola County natives are Willie Nelson, Waylon Jennings, George Jones, and Kris Kristofferson.

No country western museum would be complete without musical instruments played by the stars. More than twenty guitars are displayed around the museum, including Clint Black's black instrument and "The American," a red, white, and blue patriotic model played by Buck

Owens. There is a Gibson guitar used by Tex Ritter and a C.F. Martin 0-18 model from 1932, early in Ritter's career.

An autographed "Melody Ranch" guitar was one of thousands sold by Gene Autry to his fans from 1941 to 1955. In addition, there are three Gibson "Special" guitars, used respectively by Gene Autry, Tex Ritter, and Jimmy Wakeley. Jim Reeves played a Gibson guitar from 1952 as his career began to grow.

Other guitars in the Hall of Fame collection were artfully played by such performers as Mac Davis, Tom T. Hall, Cindy Walker, Rudy Gatlin, Rodney Crowell, Johnny Bush, Bob Lyman, Ray Price (a Gibson "Country Western" model), and Jeannie C. Riley (a C.F. Martin 0-18 1961 model).

A don't-miss item is a white guitar covered with celebrity autographs. And other instruments include Charlie Walker's mandolin, John-

The event room at the TCMHOF seats 200 at tables, or 300 in auditorium seating facing the stage.

ny Gimble's fiddle, and Jimmie Day's pedal steel guitar. In addition, there is a tambourine used on stage by Kenny Rogers, as well as a banjo played by Arkansas Slim Andrews.

Arkansas Slim was a comedian/musician who was Tex Ritter's sidekick in ten movies and public appearances for a decade. The versatile Arkansas Slim also "played" a bicycle pump and other unorthodox instruments, several of which are exhibited in his display case.

A wing in the northwest area of the museum is full of display cases devoted to the "Hall of Friends," performers from outside Texas who have contributed their talents to TCMHOF induction shows. This stellar list includes Barbara Fairchild, Dottie and Shelly West, Whisperin' Bill Anderson, Jeannie Seely, Tom T. Hall, Jan Howard, Tom Perryman, Riders in the Sky, Jim Owen, Jack Greene, Jody Miller, and Johnny Bond, a special friend and biographer of Tex Ritter. Another area salutes "14 Players who con-

tributed to Country Music Radio."

A long hallway displays the impressive plaques of the inductees, numbering fifty-six as of this writing. These plaques are identical to those presented to each performer at their induction. Each plaque is rectangular, featuring a star with a relief bust of the inductees, with a metal plate at the bottom naming the inductee and the year of their induction.

Visitors depart the museum through the gift shop, where they are handed a small map indicating how to drive to the Jim Reeves Memorial, a couple of miles east of Carthage. The route goes past a magnificent religious park, Footprints in the Sand, built around a statue of Jesus created by local sculptor Bob Harness. He crafted the splendid Tex Ritter/White Flash statuary outside the Texas Country Music Hall of Fame.

A short drive eastward along Highway 79 leads to the Jim Reeves Memorial. After his 1964 death in a plane crash, his widow, Mary, imme-

The movie theater area of the museum is ringed by eye-catching posters of films starring "Singing Cowboys."

diately arranged through Carthage attorneys to purchase land to bury Reeves in his home county amid a scenic park. A towering statue of Gentleman Jim dominates the site, and the lovely setting provides a perfect ending to a day spent at the Texas Country Music Hall of Fame.

When tourists leave the museum for their cars, they often are asked how they enjoyed their visit. Their replies frequently are one-word exclamations:

"Amazing!"
"Fascinating!"
"Awesome!"
"Wow!"

The TCMHOF jukebox is loaded with country classics, which are played free of charge by museum patrons. Introduced into honky tonks and "juke joints" during the 1920s, coin-operated jukeboxes numbered 300,000 by 1940. During World War II these music machines boomed across the nation, and jukeboxes were instrumental in the spread of country music.

The work of Jim Reeves as an announcer over KGRI in Henderson and on other stations advanced his career as a music performer. The KGRI studio and equipment of the late 1940s is reproduced in the TCMHOF museum.

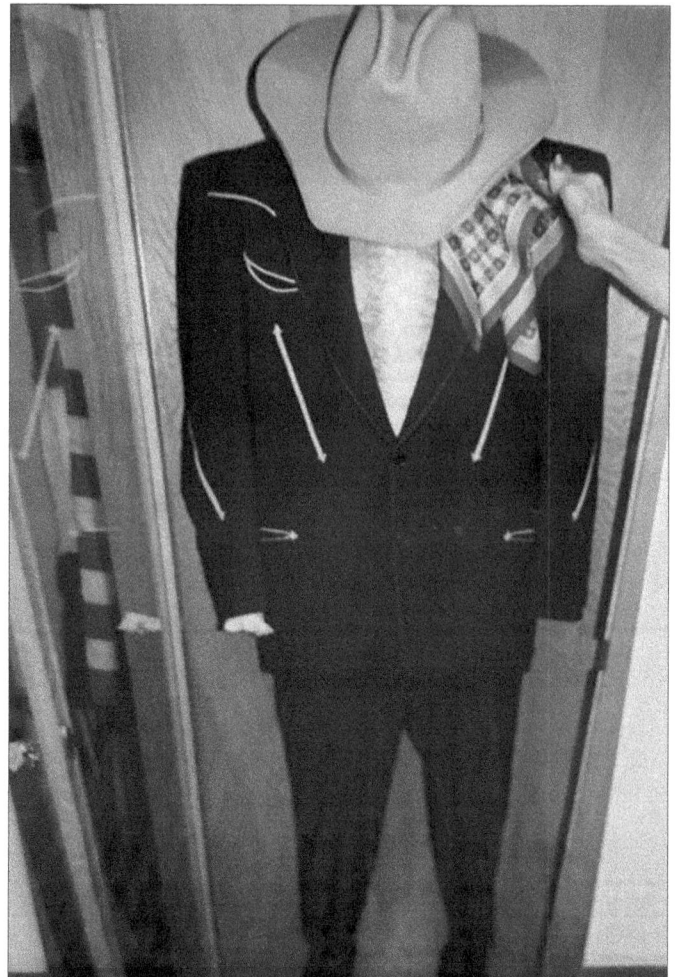

This Tex Ritter suit and hat is one of many performance costumes on display in the TCMHOF museum.

A distinctive beer can from Gilley's is part of the eclectic TCMHOF collection.

Linda Davis of Carthage provided the museum with her CHS cheerleader letter jacket and megaphone.

Bobbie Nelson presented the museum a black performance costume featuring a white piano keyboard.

Dorothy Fay Ritter toured military bases throughout the Pacific Theater with the Special Services of the US Armed Forces. Usually clad in military fatigues, she sometimes wore the dress uniform included in her TCMHOF display.

One of more than 20 guitars on display in the TCMHOF museum is a white guitar covered with celebrity autographs.

Three-time Grammy winner, Linda Davis loaned one of her awards to the TCMHOF museum.

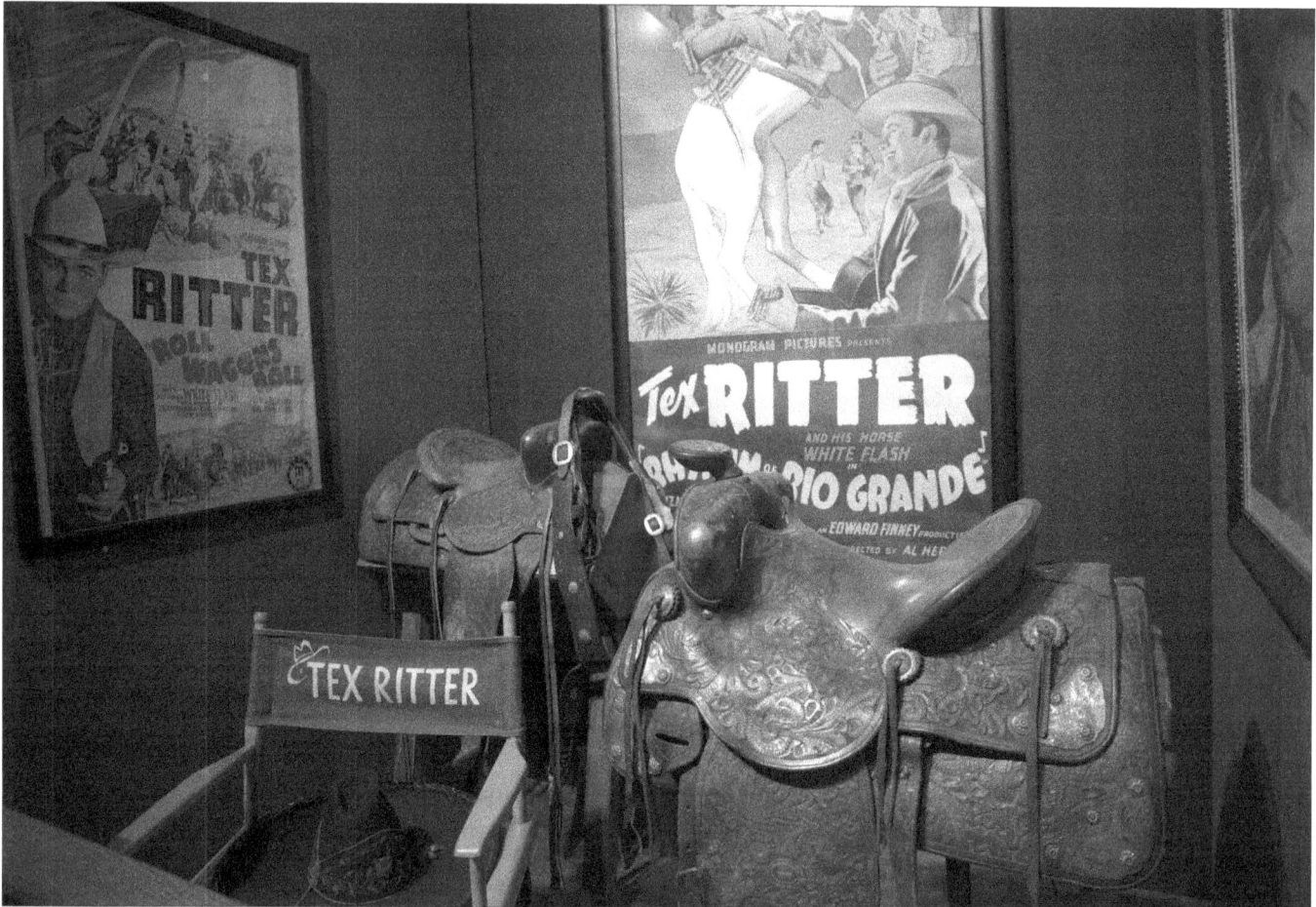

Two of several saddles in the TCMHOF display collection. "Singing Cowboys" rode horseback in Western movies and in rodeos and parades.

Two identical Hall of Fame plaques are made up for each honoree. One is given to each inductee (in this case to Kenny Rogers), and the other goes on permanent display at the TCMHOF.

A number of country stars from Texas became members of the *Grand Ole Opry*, and a striking life-size display honors Tex Ritter, Jim Reeves, Willie Nelson, Waylon Jennings, George Jones and Kris Kristofferson.

An autographed "Melody Ranch" guitar sold by Gene Autry to his fans from 1941 to 1955.

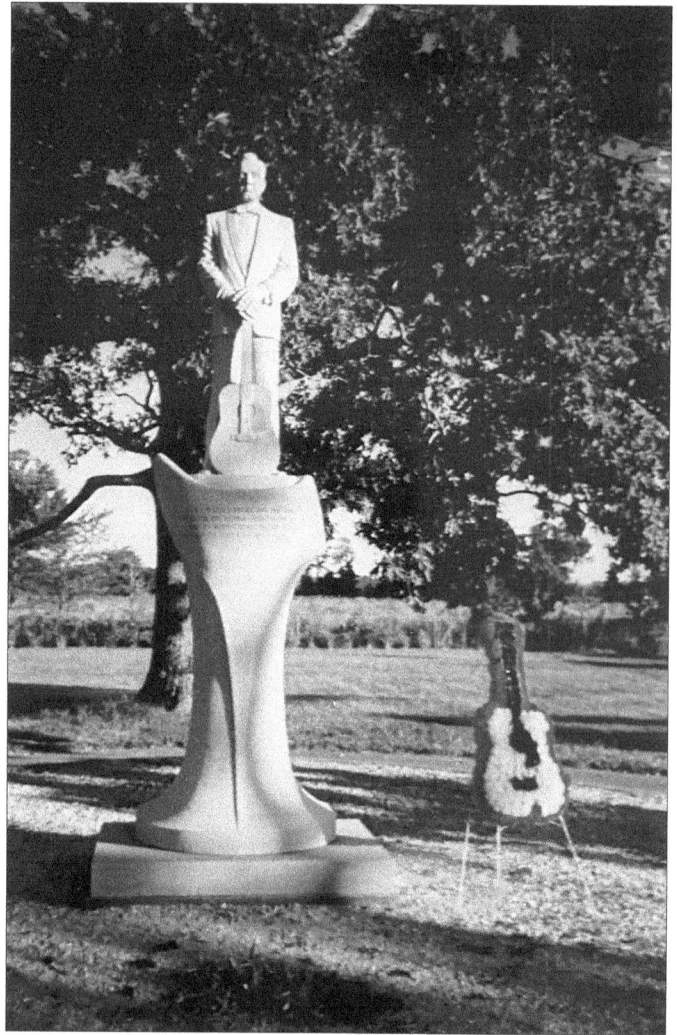

No tour of the Texas Country Music Hall of Fame is complete without a short trip east of town to the scenic memorial park which features an impressive statue of Gentleman Jim Reeves.

Chapter Two
The Growth of Texas Country Music

Any art is a reflection of life, and no art is more revealing of a people and a region than music. Texas's population has always been varied, composed of many ethnic groups. The musical background of Texas and Texans, therefore, is incredibly varied and rich. Although little is known about the music of early Native American inhabitants of the immense land that became Texas, Spanish explorers and Mexican colonists and their vibrant music live on today in Tejano strains.

Land-hungry Anglo settlers of the nineteenth century brought religious, and folk music with them to Texas, and African American slaves also

Scott Joplin from Texarkana was the greatest composer of "ragged time" music, and he became known as "The Father of Ragtime."

expressed themselves with powerful music. Germans, Czechs, French, Irish, and Jewish emigrants, along with other Europeans, added to the musical culture of Texas.

Texas produced important and gifted artists in every style of music. For example, Scott Joplin of Texarkana became known as the "Father of Ragtime," a lively new kind of syncopated popular music that swept the nation late in the nineteenth century. "Ragged time" or "ragtime" music paved the way for jazz, and Joplin, a talented pianist, became the most noted composer of ragtime. His most enduring composition was "Maple Leaf Rag."

Jack Teagarden, born in 1905 in Vernon, Texas, was an innovative instrumentalist who is regarded as the "Father of the jazz trombone." As a boy, Harry James moved with his family to Beaumont, Texas, in 1931, and at fifteen, he became a "Big Band" trumpeter with a local band. Soon he led his own band, appeared in movies, and was acclaimed by many as the most brilliant trumpeter of the Big Band era.

Mary Martin of Weatherford became a celebrated Broadway and motion picture star in musicals, creating the role of Peter Pan. (She also created Larry Hagman, her son who starred on television's *Dallas* series as the notorious J.R. Ewing.)

Buddy Holly from Lubbock, Texas, exploded onto the rock 'n' roll scene in the 1950s with such classics as "Peggy Sue," "Rave On," "It's So Easy," and "That'll Be the Day." His backup group was The Crickets, and it is thought that a band of talented British admirers named themselves the Beatles in tribute to the Texas genius whom they had seen in concert. Holly was influ-

Jack Teagarden of Vernon was famous as "The Father of the Jazz Trombone."

enced by West Texas country and western music (C&W) before switching to the new sounds of rock 'n' roll. Tragically, Holly was only twenty-two when he died in a 1959 airplane crash.

Another ill-fated Texan, Janis Joplin of Port Arthur, Texas, grew up amid a music-rich environment that included rhythm and blues (R&B), Cajun, country, and rock 'n' roll. She became a captivating folk singer known as the "Queen of Rock 'n' Roll" and the "Queen of Psychedelic Rock." Her biggest hit was "Me and Bobby Mc-Gee," written by her friend Kris Kristofferson. Sadly Janice became involved with drugs and alcohol, and she died of a heroin overdose at the age of twenty-seven in 1970.

The blues, which so strongly influenced Janis Joplin, may be traced back deep into the 1800s. African American pianists sang the blues in East Texas lumber camp taverns called "barrelhouses" because the makeshift bars were wide planks placed atop barrels. The hard-drinking patrons laughed and shouted and to be heard, and the pianists had to pound out hard-driving, up-tempo music called "barrelhouse," or "boogie-woogie," or "fast Texas blues."

Blues-singing guitarists were immensely helped by the twentieth-century inventions of microphones, amplifiers, and drum sets. Leading Texas blues artists included "Blind Lemon" Jefferson, born on a farm near Wortham, Texas, "Lightnin'" Hopkins from Centerville, Texas, "T-Bone" Walker from Linden, Texas, and Huddie "Lead Belly" Ledbetter, who was born in Louisiana but raised in Texas. Beulah "Sippie" Wallace from Houston, Texas, was a popular singer-pianist who mixed blues with boogie-woogie and gospel and jazz. Many Texas blues artists gravitated to the honky-tonks of Deep Ellum, the legendary entertainment district of west Dallas.

From the opposite end of the cultural spectrum was classical pianist Van Cliburn of Kilgore, Texas, and Fort Worth, Texas. His mother was a piano teacher who recognized that her son was a child prodigy. Van Cliburn responded to intense training, and at the age of thirteen, he was featured with the Houston Symphony Orchestra. He appeared at Carnegie Hall in New York City, where he studied at the Juilliard School of Music.

In Moscow in 1958, the twenty-three-year-old Texan won the prestigious Tchaikovsky International Piano Competition. Vaulted to worldwide fame, Van Cliburn became the most celebrated classical musician from the Lone Star State.

Another Texas musician who attained early fame was Selena Quintanilla, who was born in Lake Jackson, Texas, in 1971. Indeed, shortly after Selena's birth, two talented male artists

Mary Martin of Weatherford created the role of Peter Pan and became a brilliant star of musicals on Broadway and in motion pictures.

From Port Arthur emerged Janis Joplin as the Queen of Rock 'n' Roll and the Queen of Psychedelic Rock, although her lifestyle proved destructive.

Buddy Holly of Lubbock and his backup group, the Crickets, began by performing country and western music, but Buddy soon evolved as a major star of rock 'n' roll.

"Blind Lemon" Jefferson (1893-1929) was a blues singer and an innovative guitarist. Born sightless on a farm near Wortham, he later performed in the famous Deep Ellum district of Dallas.

Born in Lake Jackson and relocating with her family to Corpus Christi, Selena Quintanilla exploded as a superstar of Tejano music. Tragically, Selena was murdered at the age of twenty-three.

Van Cliburn, from Kilgore and Fort Worth, achieved international fame as a classical pianist.

greatly boosted Tejano music: Freddie Fender of San Benito, Texas, ("Wasted Days and Wasted Nights" and "Before the Next Teardrop Falls") and Johnny Rodriguez from Sabinal, Texas, ("Pass Me By" and "That's the Way Love Goes"). But Selena, who moved to Corpus Christi, Texas, with her family, began singing publicly as a child and became a spectacular star of previously male-dominated Tejano music.

Backed by her band, *Los Dinos — Selena y Los Dinos* [Selena and the Guys] — she sang with passion, expressing both love and pain, captivating audiences with energetic dance movements. In 1987, when she was only sixteen, Selena won the Tejano Music Award for Female Vocalist of the Year, an honor she claimed nine consecutive times. In addition, she won a Grammy in 1994 for Best Musical/American Album of the Year for *Amor Prohibido* [Forbidden Love]. Her music showed German influences, polka, jazz, r&b, country, Latin pop, and exciting technopop. Selena's emotional presentation of Tejano music has resulted in sales of 30 million records worldwide. Her signature song is *Como La Flor* [Like the Flower].

Selena became involved in designing her performance costumes, and she opened boutiques called Selena Etc. in Corpus Christi and San Antonio, with plans to expand into Mexico and elsewhere. But her life was cut tragically short in 1995 when she was shot to death by a woman who was president of her fan club.

Governor George W. Bush declared her birthday, April 16, Selena Day in Texas. Selena is remembered as the Queen of Tejano Music, the Mexican Madonna, the Chicano Elvis, and the Hispanic Marilyn Monroe.

Another successful pop singer was Jessica Simpson, born in Abilene, Texas, in 1980. Her father was a Christian youth minister; the family moved several times, and Jessica attended Richardson High School. Jessica sang with church choirs, and at seventeen, she signed with Co-lumbia Records, which helped promote her as a contrast to Britney Spears and Christina Aguilera. Her studio albums enjoyed impressive commercial success, and later she recorded music with Christian themes, as well as *Do You Know*, a country album released in 2008.

But for all of the contributions Texas artists have made to various styles of music, Texans have dominated the field of country music. This is because Texas was settled by rural Southern farmers who arrived here with their music. Music historian Gary Hartman, in *The History of Music in Texas*, points out that for these Anglo-Texans, "music played an important role in nearly every aspect of their daily lives, including dances, festivals, church services, weddings, wakes, political rallies, and numerous other events."

For dances, a country fiddler had to be lined up. A guitarist or some other instrumentalist was appreciated, but a fiddler was required. If the dancing was held in someone's farmhouse — probably on a Saturday night — furniture was cleared out of two adjoining rooms, except for chairs lined up against walls. Musicians took their places at the connecting doorway so that dance tunes could be heard clearly in the two rooms. Texas boasted more country fiddlers and more contest fiddlers than any other state.

Church music featuring gospel hymns was a vital part of pioneer Texas music. The South was regarded as the Bible Belt of the United States, and Texas proudly claimed to be the buckle on the Bible Belt.

The Spanish established more than two dozen Catholic missions in early Texas. But the Texas Revolution and the organization of the Lone Star Republic ended Catholicism's dominance of spiritual life. Baptist, Methodist, and Presbyterian missionaries promptly penetrated Texas.

Methodists were especially well organized, and by 1860 there were more than 30,000 Methodist members in the State of Texas. There were over 400 Methodist congregations and 224 "circuit riders," traveling preachers who customarily held services at perhaps three churches each Sunday.

In 1860 Texas Baptists boasted more than 500 congregations, while Presbyterians, Episcopalians, and Disciples of Christ worked energetically to build churches. After the Civil War, the Texas population grew rapidly, and so did the churches in Texas.

These churches provided vigorous preaching on Sundays and at camp meetings or "revivals." Congregations also engaged enthusiastically in hymns, sometimes backed up by a piano or an occasional organ. More commonly, rural congregations sang a cappella, often in four-part harmony.

The musical efforts of country churches were supplemented periodically by itinerant music teachers. Such a man might provide music "specials" at a morning service. Dinner on

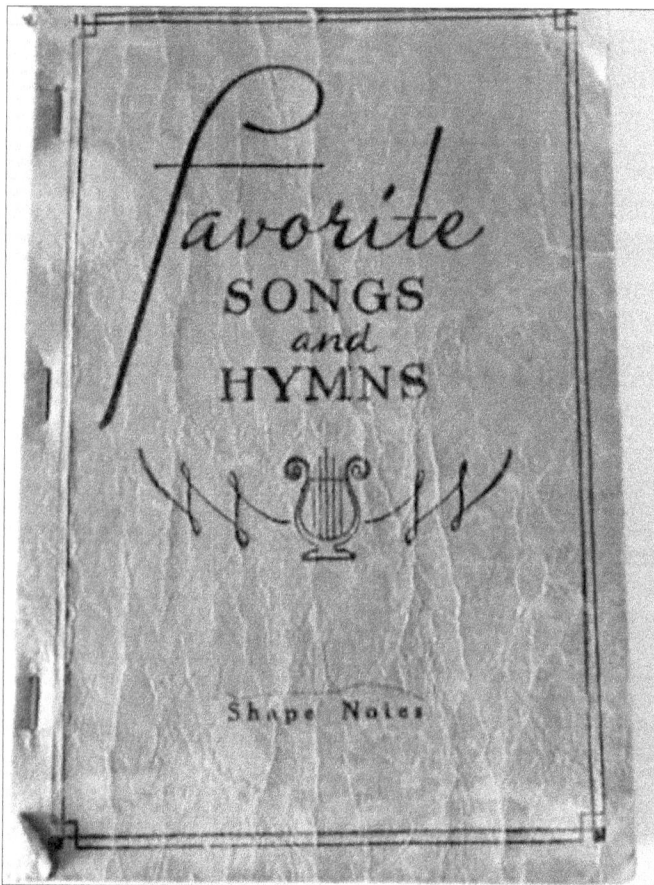

Paperback "shaped note hymnals" sold steadily in Texas churches.

the ground would follow, and the "professor" would spend the remainder of the afternoon instructing churchgoers in musical fundamentals. A basic method of teaching music centered around "shaped notes" or "shape notes," in which musical notations were simplified to as few as four shapes: circles, squares, triangles, and trapezoids. Afterward, "shaped note" paperback hymnals and sheet music would be sold to church members, or a supply of hymnals might be purchased by the church for use in services.

A longer music convention might be conducted daily for a week or even ten days in a community. "Sacred Harp" conventions (the Sacred Harp was the voice) aligned men and women in four groups for strong four-part harmony in the community "sings." Armed with shaped note hymnals, families or groups of neighbors could gather around a home pump organ or piano for a Saturday night "sing." At one point, with rampant underfunding of the state's schools, it is likely that more Texans could read music (the shape-note version) than words.

V.O. Stamps was born in 1892 in Upshur County, Texas. He attended music schools, worked for a music company, and became a gospel singer. He established the V.O. Stamps Music Company in Jacksonville, Texas, in 1924. Three years later, with a friend, J.R. Baxter, the organization expanded to the Stamps-Baxter Music and Printing Company, and headquarters soon were moved to Dallas. Stamps-Baxter soon became active in songwriting and music publishing and in conducting shape-note workshops.

In 1936 the Stamps Quartet began a daily noon broadcast over KRLD Radio in Dallas, leading off each program with their famous theme song, "Give the World a Smile." Demands for personal appearances became so great that the company began to send out a dozen "Stamps Quartets." The Stamps-Baxter Company widely popularized Southern gospel music while becoming the

The Stamps Quartet ca. 1925 (L to R) Otis Deaton, Henry Long, Edgar Goslup and Theo Casey. V.O. Stamps from Upshur County established the V.O. Stamps Music Company and the popular Stamps Quartet.

nation's leading company in the field.

The popularity of the Stamps Quartet led to similar groups based in Texas, notably the Chuck Wagon Gang and the Ranger Quartet. Brothers Vernon and Arnold Hyles grew up singing church music in their hometown of Italy, Texas, in Ellis County.

After attending the Stamps-Baxter School of Music in Dallas, the brothers formed a gospel quartet. In 1935 Gov. James Allred appointed the popular group honorary Texas Rangers, with the assignment of touring thirteen states as the Texas Rangers Quartet — ambassadors for the upcoming Texas Centennial Celebration to be held in 1936 at the State Fair in Dallas. Featuring Arnold Hyles as "The World's Loudest Basso Profundo," the group soon shortened their name to the Ranger Quartet.

Gifted showmen and tireless travelers, the Rangers became the first gospel quartet to earn a living solely by performing, with no side jobs during the week. By 1949 the Ranger Quartet had made over 10,000 live radio broadcasts, performed 5,000 stage appearances, and driven more than 1.5 million miles.

The Chuck Wagon Gang originally was a Carter family group (unrelated to folk music singers A.P. Carter, Maybelle Carter, Sara Carter, June Carter Cash, and other relatives). The Texas Carters was organized in 1935, consisting initially of Dad Carter, Rose Carter Karnes, Ernest Carter, and Effie Carter Gordon Davis. After broadcasting over KFYO Radio in Lubbock, in 1936, the Carters moved to WBAP Radio in Fort Worth, where they acquired the Chuck Wagon Gang label. The Chuck Wagon Gang recorded for Columbia Records for thirty-nine years. They appeared on stage at Carnegie Hall, the Hollywood Bowl, and the *Grand Ole Opry*.

Gary Hartman pointed out that such groups as the Chuck Wagon Gang "blended religious music with country and other styles." Indeed, Country music spread across the nation during World War II, as rural Southerners migrated to war plant jobs in the Northeast, Chicago, and California. In Hollywood, country and western music (c&w) had been popularized in horse operas since the 1930s.

Marion T. Slaughter from Jefferson, Texas, was popularly known as Vernon Dalhart. He became the first artist to record country and western music.

The first successful "Singing Cowboy" was Gene Autry from Tioga, a farm town in north Texas where he began singing as a boy in his grandfather's church choir.

Members of the Rangers Quartet were appointed honorary Texas Rangers by Gov. James Allred.

Of course, the "West" in country and western music did not originate with Hollywood movies. Texas gave the West the cowboy, and the cowboy would become the world's number one folk hero. Working cowboys made music around campfires, in bunkhouses, and while riding night herd. Nightherders tried to keep the cattle calm so they would not stampede, and the cattle were soothed by music.

Unfortunately, the only music that many young cowboys knew was from boyhood church singing. So drovers sang church hymns, or they adapted cowboy ballads to hymn music. The most famous cowboy ballad was "Little Joe the Wrangler," and it was sung to the tune of the classic hymn, "Lily of the Valley."

The first artist to record popular country and western was a musically talented Texan from Jefferson. Marion T. Slaughter was born in 1883. Young Slaughter grew up herding cows on the family ranch and singing at community functions. He learned to sing harmony and play the harmonica, and he became an expert whistler, a musical ability he would use in his recording career.

Slaughter's father was killed in a shootout behind a Jefferson saloon. During summers, the teenage Slaughter worked as a cowboy in West Texas, but after moving to Dallas with his widowed mother, he studied at the Dallas Conservatory of Music.

With his teachers' encouragement, Slaughter relocated to New York City with his wife and small son in his mid-twenties. Slaughter caught on with an opera troupe, and when he earned a feature role in *Girl of the Golden West*, he adapted a stage name from two West Texas towns, Vernon and Dalhart. Vernon Dalhart performed as a tenor in *The Merry Widow* and *Madam Butterfly* and *H.M.S. Pinafore*. And by 1915, he commenced an astounding recording career. Using over 130 pseudonyms — although he remained best-known as Vernon Dalhart — he worked for almost every recording company in the nation, as well as a large number in England. Recording nearly every type of music, he cut well over 5,000 sides.

His greatest hit was first recorded in 1924. "The Wreck of the Old 97," was enormously popular with country people, who loved songs about trains. Even more successful was "The Prisoner's Song," an old folk tune that Slaughter managed to copyright. Recorded by Slaughter on at least fifty record labels, the song became the first country million-seller and convinced the industry to welcome country artists. Throughout his career "Vernon Dalhart" sold 25 million records during an era when the American population was no more than one-quarter of today.

As the career of Vernon Dalhart peaked, Hollywood's "Singing Cowboys" brought country and western music to a new level of popularity. For the first three decades of the twentieth century, Hollywood produced silent Westerns by the hundreds, but by the time sound was introduced to motion pictures in the late 1920s, the Western formula was growing stale. Early sound Westerns, in the interest of economy, did not insert background music. But the dialogue was simple and cliched, and most cowboy stars delivered their lines awkwardly.

Although young fans came to Westerns for action, not acting, the action seemed flat without the exciting musical strains provided by silent theater pianists. Cowboy hero Ken Maynard, who was a fiddler as well as a superb horseman, tried musical interludes in his films, and so did young John Wayne. But unfortunately, Wayne's singing voice had to be dubbed, and his experiment as "Singin' Sandy" proved brief.

But Maynard engaged Gene Autry, a Chicago radio star from Texas, to deliver musical numbers in his movies. Gene Autry was born in 1907 in Tioga, a small farm town about fifty miles north of Dallas.

Gene's grandfather was a Baptist preacher,

and he put the boy on the front row of his choir. After the family moved to Oklahoma, Gene learned to play the guitar. The Tulsa radio station KVOO aired Gene as "Oklahoma's Singing Cowboy," and soon, he advanced to Chicago's powerful radio station, WSM, as star of the *National Barn Dance*. "That Silver Haired Daddy of Mine," co-written by Gene, headlined the recording industry's first album to go gold.

After going to Hollywood in 1934 to sing in two Ken Maynard movies, Gene suddenly was plugged in to star in a 1935 twelve-part serial, *The Phantom Empire*, when Ken was too drunk to start filming. Although Gene was a better singer than actor, he was a phenomenal success with youthful audiences, many of whom found him a smiling big-brother image.

Gene was rushed from one film to another, and in 1936 — the year of the Texas Centennial — two Autry Westerns were released that were centered on the Lone Star State. *The Big Show* placed Gene and his horse Champion — and his comic sidekick, Smiley Burnette (a brilliant musician) — at the Centennial Celebration in Dallas.

Gene, Champion, and Smiley were back with the Texas Rangers in *Ride Ranger Ride*. (The movie's title song was adapted by the Lions Clubs of America as "Roar Lions Roar.") Hollywood's first "singing cowboy" went on to star in ninety-one Western movies.

Autry's success in Hollywood created a demand for more singing cowboys and a talent scout located Tex Ritter in New York City. Woodard Maurice Ritter, born in 1905, was raised on an East Texas cotton farm in Panola County. Country culture was deeply embedded in the farm boy, as reflected by such later recordings as "De Boll Weevil," a cotton field ballad he learned from African American farm hands, and "On That H and TC Line," a train song: "On that H and TC Line / Old East Texas sure looks fine / Drop me off just anywhere / Tenaha, Timp-

son, Bobo, and Blair." Tenaha and Timpson were East Texas farm towns about ten miles apart, while Bobo and Blair were water stops alongside the railroad. But during World War II, at army camps worldwide, soldiers needing to roll a ten in a crap game would shout at the dice, "Tenaha, Timpson, Bobo, and Blair!" Thus advertised, the growing fame of the song phrase resulted in another hit for Tex Ritter. And the folk song "Rye Whiskey" also became a Ritter hit.

Aspiring to become a lawyer, Ritter spent five years at the University of Texas. But as the years passed, he became more focused on his activities with the University Glee Club — he twice served as president — than on his studies.

Conductor Oscar Fox provided vocal training for Ritter's rich bass voice and instruction in guitar and sight-reading. Faculty member John A. Lomax, who grew up in Bosque Coun-

Panola County's Tex Ritter studied music through the University of Texas Glee Club, then followed a performing career to Broadway, network radio, Hollywood, countless personal appearances, television, and recording activities which produced 460 "covers."

The beautiful Dorothy Fay Southworth co-starred with Tex Ritter in four Westerns. Tex and Dorothy were married in 1941 and became the parents of two sons, Tom and John.

ty, Texas, on a farm adjacent to a branch of the Chisholm Trail, began writing down cowboy ballads. As an adult, Lomax traveled 200,000 miles — often accompanied by his son Alan — collecting ballads and folk tunes. (John and Alan located Hudie Ledbetter in a Louisiana prison and were instrumental in securing the release of "Lead Belly" and the resumption of his performing career.)

J. Frank Dobie, another legendary faculty member, as well as an author and folklorist, along with John Lomax and Oscar Fox, encouraged Ritter's interest in the music and lore of early Texas. Specifically, they urged him to collect his own portfolio of music, and Ritter began accumulating cowboy ballads and folk songs.

In 1927 a traveling troupe came to Austin's Hancock Opera House. Law student Ritter attended every performance, and when the troupe returned to the road, he left with them as a new member of the chorus. Eventually, he wound up in New York City, where he landed other chorus roles. With his deep voice, Ritter was a natural for radio; he already had broadcast over station KPRC in Houston, and in time he would host a children's show in New York. Because of his Texas accent, fellow performers began calling Woodard Ritter "Tex."

Tex Ritter was discovered in New York City by a talent scout, and in 1936 he was flown to Hollywood to become a singing cowboy for Grand National Pictures. For the next ten years, Tex starred in sixty horse operas. He sang cowboy songs and galloped across the screen on White Flash. Tall and rangy, he was convincing in fight scenes. Tex cut records and made countless personal appearances between films, and his popularity soared.

The third prominent singing cowboy was Roy Rogers, who was Leonard Slye from Duck Run, Ohio. Roy Rogers ultimately made eighty-nine films and reigned as the "King of the Cowboys." The top three singing cowboys were Gene Autry, Tex Ritter, and Roy Rogers.

Roy was the only one of the three not from Texas, but he married a Texan, Dale Evans. Roy's frequent co-star, she was beautiful and a gifted singer. Before becoming Dale Evans and the "Queen of the West," she was Francis Octavia Smith from Uvalde, Texas, and Italy, Texas. Among other compositions, she wrote "Happy Trails," the theme song of Roy and Dale, who co-starred from 1951 through 1957 on television on *The Roy Rogers Show*.

During the same period that the singing cowboys were disseminating country and western music, a dynamic new sound called "Western swing" or "Texas swing" was being popularized by Bob Wills and his Texas Playboys. Wills was born near Kosse, Texas, in 1905, the oldest of ten children. When Bob was eight, the family moved to Turkey in West Texas. Bob's father, John Wills,

Dale Evans married her frequent co-star, Roy Rogers, the "King of the Cowboys." Dale, who was born and raised in Texas, achieved stardom as the "Queen of the West." Gabby Hayes (far right) was a also a frequent co-star.

was a farmer and a country fiddler who played for ranch dances. John taught Bob to fiddle, using his son as a backup, but Bob soon was playing lead.

While young Bob Wills entertained with traditional country music, he became captivated by the lively jazz sounds of the Roaring Twenties. He eagerly sang and played the blues, also incorporating strains of polka and ragtime, along with pop and swing.

In 1929 Wills moved to Fort Worth, where he met another innovative musician, Milton Brown from Stephenville, Texas. Within two years, Wills, Brown, and Herman Arnspiger from Van Alstyne, Texas, were playing on the radio as the Light Crust Doughboys, advertising the Light Crust Flour of their sponsor, the Burrus Mill and Elevator Company. The toe-tapping diversity of their music created Western swing.

Milton Brown organized his own band, the Musical Brownies, in 1932, but four years later, he suffered fatal injuries in an auto crash. Like Brown, Bob Wills left the Doughboys and formed the Texas Playboys in 1933, although the Light Crust Doughboys continued performing into the twenty-first century. Meanwhile, Bob Wills added horns and drums, and more fiddles to the Texas Playboys. In the era of Benny Goodman and Glenn Miller, with popular music dominated by big band swing, Bob Wills established the Texas Playboys as country's largest band, and he became known as the "Father of Western Swing."

Bob moved to Tulsa, Okla., in 1934, enjoying great success over KVOO Radio and with recordings such as "New San Antonio Rose," "Faded Love," and "Lone Star Rag." His attempts to break into Western movies were unsuccessful

Bob Wills, born in Kosse in Central Texas and raised at Turkey in the Texas Panhandle, was a superb fiddler and an innovative musician who developed "Western Swing" during the Big Band era. The first film appearance of Bob Wills and his Texas Playboys was in a 1940 Tex Ritter movie, *Take Me Back to Oklahoma*.

until 1940 when Tex Ritter arranged for Wills to co-star with him in *Take Me Back to Oklahoma*. Bob and the Playboys performed six numbers in the film, and during the next two years, eleven horse operas lensed by Columbia Pictures featured Wills and his Western swing bang.

Until his Western movies, most Bob Wills fans had never seen him. They listened to his music over the radio and on records, but now they could actually watch Bob Wills and his Texas Playboys in performance on movie screens. The same popularity enhancement already had been enjoyed by Gene Autry, Tex Ritter, and other singing cowboys (after all, television and music videos did not yet exist).

"To me, country music is from your heart and soul." These words came from Ernest Tubb, reflecting back on a long career. "E.T." was born in 1914 in Ellis County, Texas. He learned to play the guitar and became a yodeler, one of many young musicians who attempted to copy the yodeling style of Jimmie Rodgers.

A tonsillectomy changed the yodeler to a bass, but in 1941 he recorded his own composition, "Walking the Floor Over You," which became a million-seller. Tubb appeared in movies, and in 1943 he joined the *Grand Ole Opry*, performing for four decades. E.T. and his Texas Troubadours toured constantly, and country music indeed poured from his heart and soul.

With his large band and other members of his entourage, Bob Wills usually traveled with more than a score of fellow artists in a bus which now is on display in Turkey.

Lefty Frizzell from Corsicana, Texas, began singing in honky-tonks as a teenager. His plaintive voice and unique phrasing led to a recording career that started in 1950 when he was twenty-two. "If You've Got the Money Honey, I've Got the Time" and "I Love You a Thousand Ways" were among his most memorable hits. The success of rock 'n' roll in the 1950s cut into his record sales, but he remained popular with live audiences while influencing other singers. Unfortunately, however, Frizzell led a destructive lifestyle, and he died at forty-seven in 1975.

A gifted contemporary of Lefty Frizzell's was James Travis Reeves. Like William Orville Frizzell, Reeves would become known by a performance sobriquet, "Gentleman Jim." Reeves was born in 1923 on a farm in Panola County, and at Carthage High School, he was a pitching star on the baseball team. Although recruited for the University of Texas baseball squad, Reeves remained at U.T. only briefly in 1942 before finding wartime employment in a Houston shipyard. After the war, the minor leagues of professional baseball exploded with growth, and Reeves pitched a couple of seasons in the Class C East Texas League for Marshall and Henderson.

In Henderson, Reeves worked as a deejay at KGRI Radio. He had learned to play guitar as a little boy, and from time to time on the air, he would pick up his guitar and sing a country tune. KGRI listeners became immediate fans of his music, and he began entertaining in the East Texas area with a small band.

In 1949 Reeves started recording on small labels. A 1953 release, "Mexican Joe," was hugely popular. By this time, Reeves was an announcer on Shreveport's Louisiana Hayride, and one night he performed "Mexican Joe." He was called back for six encores and became a star on the Hayride. Within two years, he was invited to the *Grand Ole Opry*, and at the same time, he was signed by RCA Victor.

A series of his records included "Four Walls" and "He'll Have to Go." Reeves drifted away from his early hillbilly style, dropping fiddles and steel guitars from his backup band and enjoying the support of a melodious chorus on his recordings. His baritone voice often was described as "velvet," and he rapidly built crossover popularity. In 1959, for example, "He'll Have to Go" soared to number one on the country charts, while reaching number two on the

Early in his career Bob Wills was a charter member of the Light Crust Doughboys, a country band organized by future Texas governor Pappy Lee O'Daniel to advertise his Fort Worth flour mill, Burris Mills. The Light Crust Doughboys enjoyed a long career as an iconic Texas band.

pop charts.

Country music authority Bill C. Malone, author of *Country Music U.S.A.*, stated, "Reeves had probably the greatest ability to appeal to popular audiences while maintaining a country identity."

During the late 1950s and early 1960s, Gentleman Jim toured the European continent, Scandinavia, and South Africa, where he headlined a movie, *Kimberley Jim*. But with his career steadily reaching new heights, Reeves was only forty-one in 1964 when he flew his light plane into a storm near Nashville and perished in the resulting crash. Three years later, he was voted into the Country Music Hall of Fame, and his record company cleverly marketed his unreleased material, scoring numerous hits long after his death.

Hank Thompson was born in Waco, Texas,

in 1925, the same decade as Reeves and Frizzell, but he was blessed with a much longer performing career than these noted contemporaries. As a boy, Hank admired the *Grand Ole Opry* and Gene Autry movies, and he began to play and sing, landing a local radio gig while still in high school.

He organized a superb band, the Brazos Valley Boys, and Tex Ritter helped Hank arrange a contract with Capitol Records. Hank Thompson recorded hits in five decades, ultimately selling more than 60 million records. The first country artist to play Las Vegas, Hank also headlined the first color television telecast of a country syndicated program, *The Hank Thompson Show*.

Another product of the 1920s in Texas was Ray Price, born in Perryville, Texas, in 1926. During his boyhood, Ray liked all styles of popular music. He began performing as a honky-

Ernest Tubb from Ellis County enjoyed a long career as a headliner of the *Grand Ole Opry*.

A honky tonk singer with a plaintive vocal style, Lefty Frizzell from Corsicana exerted a strong influence on other performers.

Buck Owens moved from Texas to California, where he developed the popular Bakersfield Sound, before starring on television's *Hee Haw*.

Panola County farm boy Travis Reeves became Gentleman Jim Reeves, a superstar with enormous crossover appeal.

tonk singer but moved steadily into pop-country. From radio shows in Abilene, Texas, Price joined the *Big D Jamboree*, broadcast live from Dallas. Relocating to Nashville in 1951, Price became friends with Hank Williams.

After Hank's death in 1953, his Drifting Cowboys were recruited by Price to become the Cherokee Cowboys. In decades to come, Price recorded a string of hits, including "Release Me," "Heartaches by the Number," "Make the World Go Away," and "For the Good Times."

Jimmy Dean was born in 1928 in Plainview, Texas. A tall, confident performer, he worked on local radio stations as a young man before hosting a television show, *Town and Country Jubilee*. He wrote a ballad about a folk-hero coal miner, "Big Bad John." Released by Columbia Records in 1961, "Big Bad John" was an enormous success, reaching number one on both the country and pop charts. While elevating his career to network television and motion pictures, he earned additional fortune and fame through his Jimmy Dean Meat Company.

Born a year after Jimmy Dean, Buck Owens spent his first eight years in Sherman, Texas, before the family moved to Arizona. Buck's skills as a performer brought him responsive audiences and radio appearances. In 1951 he moved to Bakersfield, Calif., where he played with several bands, experimenting with styles from Western swing to r 'n' b, country to pop, to rockabilly.

Buck met Merle Haggard and other innovative musicians, and Owens was a key figure in developing the distinctive "Bakersfield Sound." Buck organized a fine backup band called the "Buckaroos," During the 1960s, he recorded twenty number one hits on the *Billboard* charts. He headed a syndicated television show, *Buck Owens Ranch*, before becoming co-host of the nationally popular *Hee Haw*.

Several men destined to become notable artists made their nativity debuts in Texas during the 1930s. Willie Nelson was born in 1933 in Ab-

bott, Texas, a small cotton-farming town, where he and his sister Bobbie were raised by their grandparents. Willie sang gospel music in the Baptist church, and he listened to Western swing and jazz and honky-tonk, as well as blues from African American cotton field laborers.

When he was six, his grandfather gave him a guitar and taught him chords, and within three years, he began playing with a band. Willie became an excellent instrumentalist, often playing with polka bands from nearby Czech communities, while Bobbie was an exceptional pianist.

Willie wrote songs, worked as a deejay, and moved to Nashville in 1960. He played bars with Ray Price's Cherokee Cowboys, began to write such hits as "Crazy," "Hello Walls," and "Funny How Time Slips Away," and in 1965, he was invited to join the *Grand Ole Opry*.

Despite his success, Willie's efforts as a singer were frustrated. By 1972 he had left Nashville and moved back to Texas. He ditched his clean-cut, neatly-dressed Nashville image for a bearded look with long hair braids, a headband, and tattered jeans. He was welcomed back to the Texas honky-tonk circuit. He was a special hit in Austin, with its Armadillo World Headquarters and a youthful music scene featuring *Austin City Limits*, which Willie headlined in its 1975 pilot episode for PBS.

His 1973 album, *Red Headed Stranger*, featured the mega-hit "Blue Eyes Crying in the Rain." In 1979 *The Electric Horseman*, starring Robert Redford and Jane Fonda, launched Willie Nelson's movie and television acting career while bringing him one of his greatest hits: "Mamas, Don't Let Your Babies Grow Up to Be Cowboys." A string of hits and awards established Willie as a Lone Star musical icon while bringing him international fame.

George Jones was born in 1931 in Saratoga, Texas, in the Big Thicket. He sang in his mother's church choir while listening avidly to the *Grand Ole Opry*. In 1942 the family moved to Beaumont, Texas, where George's father could work in war-related industries. Young George sang and played his guitar on the teeming streets of Beaumont, and by the age of fourteen, he was singing on local radio stations. During a 1951-53 enlistment in the Marines, Jones was stationed primarily in California, where he found other opportunities to sing.

Following his discharge, Jones was on the cast of the *Louisiana Hayride* for three years before joining the *Grand Ole Opry* in 1956. His first number one hit was "White Lightning," and he remained a honky-tonk singer and a powerful hard country performer.

Bill C. Malone described the "heart-wrenching complaints of unrequited or broken love" in his music and his "searing emotional singing," which emphasized, "the enunciation of words either with rounded, open-throated precision or through clenched teeth."

Waylon Jennings was born in 1937 near the South Plains town of Littlefield, Texas, and was destined to become a leader of the "Outlaw" movement of country music. Waylon's hard-working father sang and played the guitar for relaxation, influencing the talented boy with his love of traditional country & western. At thirteen, Waylon organized a band, the Texas Longhorns, and led his little backup group to appearances on KVOW Radio in Littlefield.

Jennings began deejay work at twelve, and six years later, while working at KDAW Radio in Lubbock, Waylon became friends with Buddy Holly — soon to become a rock 'n roll idol. Holly engaged Jennings as a bass player in 1959, but Buddy was killed in a plane crash within a few weeks, along with "Big Bopper" J.P. Richardson and Richie Valens. Jennings was supposed to fly on the plane, but he agreed to give his seat to Richardson.

During the 1960s, Jennings achieved recording success in Nashville. But he became increasingly uncomfortable with the lavish production

Waylon Jennings from the Texas Panhandle was a sideman for Buddy Holly, then achieved recording success as a solo performer before becoming a leader of the Outlaw Movement.

values of the period, and he moved back toward the simpler, more direct sound of traditional country. Willie Nelson and other artists also were leaning in this direction, and in 1976, Willie, Waylon, and his wife, Jessi Colter, released *Wanted: The Outlaws*, the first-ever platinum country album. As a foremost member of outlaw oountry, Waylon Jennings was a star performer for the rest of his life.

No artist born in the 1930s enjoyed greater commercial success than Kenny Rogers. Born in 1938 in Houston, Rogers was popular during the 1960s as a folk singer with the New Christy Minstrels and the First Edition. Performing as a solo act in 1977, Rogers scored an enormous hit with "Lucille," which he followed with such other hits as "The Gambler," "Lady," and "Coward of the County." After that, he took his talents to television and motion pictures and remained

A native of Houston, Barbara Mandrell enjoyed a level of success attained by few other women in country music.

a major pop-country performer.

Another star of pop-country was Barbara Mandrell. Born in 1948 in Houston, she sang in church and learned to play numerous instruments. By her teens, Barbara was appearing onstage with major country stars, and soon a recording career led to such memorable hits as "I Was Country When Country Wasn't Cool," "Sleeping Single in a Double Bed," and "Woman to Woman."

In addition, Barbara brought beauty and high-energy performance gifts to the stage and her television variety show, featuring her sisters, Louise and Irlene Mandrell.

Another talented and hard-working Texas lady was Tanya Tucker, born in 1958 in Seminole, Texas. Tanya's older sister, La Costa, enjoyed a level of success as a country singer. But Tanya exploded to stardom at the age of thirteen with "Delta Dawn," followed by other hits including "What's Your Mama's Name" and "San Antonio Stroll."

The teen sensation often made explicit mentions of sex and controversial behavior in her songs, and later she had a turbulent relationship with country star Glen Campbell. Tanya made an effort to switch her career to rock 'n roll but soon turned back to country, thereby remaining a role model for determined young ladies aspiring to succeed in country music.

Another highly successful female artist was Lee Ann Womack, born in 1966 in Jacksonville, Texas. Her father was a school administrator and a part-time deejay. At the radio station, Lee Ann helped select records to be played, and she fell in love with traditional country music. She attended South Plains College in Levelland, Texas, one of the nation's first schools to offer courses in country music. Later she transferred to Belmont University in Nashville, where she studied the business side of music.

After college, Lee Ann married and started a family, but she also wrote and performed country music. In 2000 Womack achieved major success with the album and the title song, *I Hope You*

Grammy-winner Linda Davis, like Tex Ritter and Jim Reeves, is a native of Panola County.

Dance.

Linda Davis from Panola County is a contemporary of Womack's. As a girl, Linda sang in church, learning to play piano and guitar. After a year of college, she followed her dream to Nashville to be a country singer. In addition to musical talent, Linda had a sweet and effervescent personality, and she made friends from Kenny Rogers to Reba McEntire.

With McEntire, she won a Grammy for their number one hit in 1993, "Does He Love You." Two more Grammy Awards followed in 2017 for Best Contemporary Christian Album and Best Contemporary Christian Performance.

Clint Black from Katy, Texas, began playing guitar and harmonica, as well as writing songs, during his teen years. After signing with RCA, Black's debut album, *Killin' Time*, was released in 1989. He wrote or co-wrote every song on the album, and five of these songs charted at number one. In 1991 Black became a member of the *Grand Ole Opry*, and by the following year, his first two traditionalist albums had sold a combined five million copies. Black also began appearing in motion pictures and on television shows, and in 1996 he became only the fourth country singer to earn a star on the Hollywood Walk of Fame.

No Texas artist has done more to re-invigorate traditional country, especially cowboy songs and c&w, than Michael Martin Murphey. Born in 1945 in Dallas, he was raised in Big D, graduating from high school and beginning his performing career there. But from his childhood, he visited the ranches of his grandfather and uncle, riding horses and soaking up cowboy culture from oldtimers. As a teenager, he formed a band and began playing in clubs around the city. He had written songs since he was a schoolboy and learned to play guitar, banjo, piano, mandolin, and harmonica.

Murphey attended North Texas State University in Denton before transferring to the University of California, Los Angeles. He promptly became involved in the L.A. music scene, performing folk music and composing hit songs for The Monkees, Kenny Rogers, and the First Edition.

But in 1971, Murphey gravitated back to Texas, becoming part of outlaw country and releasing his first album in 1972. The following year, his second album, *Cosmic Cowboy Souvenir*, coined an instantly popular phrase in Austin: "Cosmic Cowboy." In the ensuing years, Murphey moved beyond outlaw country to write and sing about the Old West, cowboy tunes, and gunfighter ballads. In 1990 his album, *Cowboy Songs*, went gold, and Murphey followed with a succession of similar albums.

Murphey appeared with symphony orchestras, beginning with the New Mexico Symphony

Michael Martin Murphey from Dallas gravitated to ranch life, and as a musician/songwriter he has reinvigorated traditional cowboy sounds.

in *A Night in the American West*, ultimately bringing this popular program to New York City, Las Vegas, and Washington D.C., in concert with the National Symphony Orchestra. A 1995 album, *Sagebrush Symphony*, was recorded live with the San Antonio Symphony.

For years Murphey toured during December with a delightful Western-themed Christmas program. His traditional and original Christmas songs are reflected in two albums: *Cowboy Christmas*, *Cowboy Songs II* ("The Cowboy Christmas Ball," "The Christmas Trail," "Two-Step Round the Christmas Tree") and *Acoustic Christmas Carols*, *Cowboy Christmas II*.

American Cowboy Magazine placed Murphey among the Top 50 Greatest Country and Western singers. In 2004 he was inducted into the Western Heritage Music Association Hall of Fame. Murphey was presented Western Heritage Awards from the National Cowboy Hall of Fame six times, and he was honored with a Wrangler Award induction into the National Cowboy Hall of Fame.

Mac Davis was born in 1942 and raised in Lubbock, listening almost solely to country music until he reached his teens. After high school, he left Lubbock ("in his rear view mirror"), organized a rock 'n roll band in Atlanta, Georgia, and began to make his mark as a songwriter.

Elvis Presley recorded Mac's tunes, and so did numerous other noted artists. As a singer, Davis enjoyed crossover success, and in the 1970s, he starred in such motion pictures as *North Dallas Forty* and *The Sting II*. In addition, he hosted a television variety show on NBC, *The Mac Davis Show*, and numerous other television features; he starred in Christmas specials for several years. He was named A.M.C.'s Entertainer of the Year in 1974, and during the 1970s, he placed numerous hits on both country and pop charts.

Destined to become a stellar close harmony trio, the Gatlin Brothers — Larry, Steve, and Rudy — made their stage debut in a talent contest in Abilene in 1955. Larry was six, Steve was four, and Rudy was two. A year later, the West Texas boys won Abilene's *Cavalcade of Talent*, foreshadowing future triumphs.

The Gatlin brothers grew up with close harmony both in church and at gospel "sings," and they sang at church events and on radio stations. All three brothers went to college, and afterward, Larry joined a high-profile gospel group, the Imperials, performing with Jimmy Dean's Las Vegas show.

Larry soon moved to Nashville, where he sang backup in recording studios for Kris Kristofferson. Larry's songs were recorded by Kristofferson, Dottie West, Elvis Presley, Johnny Cash, Barbra Streisand, Tom Jones, and other artists.

Steve and Rudy also pursued music careers, touring with Tammy Wynette. After Larry secured a recording contract, with the help of Kris Kristofferson, his first number one hit was "I Just Wish You Were Someone I Love," released in 1978. The next year, recording as Larry Gatlin and the Gatlin Brothers Band, the siblings hit number one with "All the Gold in California." The Gatlins were invited to join the *Grand Ole Opry*, and they performed at the White House and at Radio City Music Hall in New York City.

Even greater musical success was enjoyed by George Strait, born in 1952 and raised, along with his older brother, at Pearsall, Texas. George's main focus was on the family ranch, where he grew up more interested in horseback riding and calf roping than in music. When George began to pay attention to music, he was attracted to the traditional sounds of George Jones, Lefty Frizzell, Hank Thompson, Ray Price, Bob Wills, Merle Haggard, and Hank Williams.

In 1971 George married his high school sweetheart, Norma Voss. George and Norma would have two children, Jenifer (tragically killed in an auto accident at the age of thirteen) and George, Jr.

After a year of college in San Marcos (the

school now is known as Texas State University), Strait served a four-year hitch in the U.S. Army. While stationed at Schofield Barracks in Hawaii, he began performing with an army-sponsored band. Following his discharge, Strait returned to San Marcos to finish an agricultural degree in ranch management.

While in college, he responded to a campus flyer and joined a country band. George became the lead singer and renamed the band Ace in the Hole. They performed in local honky tonks and bars, soon venturing as far as Huntsville and Houston. George and the Ace in the Hole Band played Western swing, developing a strong regional following.

The act opened for the Texas Playboys, but finding a record contract proved difficult because the era's preferred sound was pop country, while thirty miles north of San Marcos was Austin, the heart of the outlaw movement. Strait, a working rancher, performed in starched Wranglers, a pressed Western shirt, and a cowboy hat, his clean-cut image starkly contrasting to the scruffy outlaw look. And his music perpetuated an earlier country sound. Indeed, at the height of his enormous success, his Ace in the Hole band numbered eleven, very much in the Bob Wills and big band-Western swing tradition.

Not until 1981 did Strait sign a record contract with MCA. His first album was *Strait Country*, while the second, *Strait from the Heart*, featured his number one single, "Fool-Hearted Memory." Strait's third album, *Right or Wrong*, showcased as the old Bob Wills Western swing classic title song. Also, in 1983 *Does Fort Worth Ever Cross Your Mind* became Strait's first number one album. That same year Strait made the first of more than twenty appearances at the Houston Livestock Show and Rodeo, eventually attracting a total attendance in excess of one million. *For the Last Time: Live From the Astrodome* was a recording of the final Houston Livestock Show and Rodeo to be performed in the historic

George Strait from Pearsall achieved incomparable heights in Country music, recording more than sixty number one songs and selling over 100 million records, while setting all-time concert attendance marks.

Astrodome. Strait's performance set the record for paid attendance, 68,266, breaking the former record of 67,000 set by Selena in 1995.

Year after year, Strait produced Album of the Year and Single of the Year while garnering such awards as Top Male Vocalist and Entertainer of the Year. A Special Achievement Award was made in 2003 by the Academy of Country Music in recognition of Strait's fifty number one songs. As of this writing, his total of number one hits is an all-time record of sixty-one. Strait's best-selling album is *Pure Country* (1992), which sold 6 million copies, and he has sold more than 100 million records worldwide.

Strait announced in 2012 that he was retiring from touring. His Cowboy Rides Away Tour, conducted in 2013 (twenty-one concerts) and 2014 (twenty-six concerts), were scheduled to be his last. All venues sold within hours of the announcement. The tour's final appearance at AT&T Stadium in Arlington, Texas, in June 2014 drew 104,793 fans, breaking the thirty-three-year-old record for the largest indoor concert in

North America (in 1981, the Rolling Stones produced an attendance of 87,500 in the New Orleans Superdome). Then, there was a best-selling album; *The Cowboy Rides Away: Live From AT&T Stadium*.

With the spectacular success of The Cowboy Rides Away Tour, it was almost an inevitable response to fan enthusiasm for George Strait to continue making selected personal appearances. Dickies Arena in Fort Worth — an entertainment center of Strait's home state — has been especially attractive, along with the T-Mobile Arena in Las Vegas. *Strait to Las Vegas* is a theme that has produced thirty total shows. "Strait to South Bend" brought the "King of Country Music" to Notre Dame Stadium, and there have been exciting appearances in San Antonio, Kansas City, and at New Braunfels' legendary Gruene Hall.

One of the greatest country superstars of all time, George Strait has propelled the traditionalist sounds of Texas country music for more than four decades. Texas has produced gifted artists in a vast panorama of musical styles. Still, as fan response to George Strait proves, the country sound — cowboy songs — maintains a dominant and lasting strain of Texas music. In fact, there are so many stellar country artists from the Lone Star State that it seemed essential to establish a Texas Country Music Hall of Fame and Museum.

Chapter Three
Birth of the Texas Country Music Hall of Fame

"I didn't know anything about getting a museum started or how to do it," recalled Tommie Ritter Smith, who founded the Tex Ritter Museum and, not long afterward, the Texas Country Music Hall of Fame. "I had to learn how to be a 'museum person.' But I had great incentive. I wanted to honor Tex Ritter and Jim Reeves. The museum was a labor of love."

Tommie Ritter is a native of Panola County. A pretty and vivacious redhead, she was a drum major of the Carthage High School band. And Tommie was a proud member of the large Ritter clan.

Tex Ritter had moved away from Panola County with his immediate family when he was still in high school. But the recording and movie star often was on the road with his band — Tex was known as "Hollywood's Most Traveled Performer" — and as often as possible, he drove into Panola County to visit relatives and friends. Although Tommie Ritter was a cousin to the genial performer, she saw him often enough to call him "Uncle Tex."

Jim Reeves was a family friend who sometimes hunted in Colorado with Tommie's father. Following one Colorado expedition, Tommie met the hunting party at the old Carthage ice house. While Tommie's father and Jim's older brothers unloaded the meat, Jim produced a guitar, sat down, and began strumming and singing country tunes.

As a young woman, Tommie heard a lot of country and western music, and she visited Gilley's in Houston, Billy Bob's in Fort Worth, the Reo Palm Isle in Longview, and other lively country and western venues. Not long after her appointment as director of the Panola Coun-

ty Chamber of Commerce, Tommie became involved in a project to develop a video on the history of Panola County. Tommie agreed to put together material on Tex Ritter and Gentleman Jim Reeves. Unfortunately, both of these members of Nashville's Country Music Hall of Fame were deceased. Still, Tommie contacted their families for information and artifacts and permission to use stories and images of the two stars in a video.

During these negotiations, Tommie was able to interest John Ritter, the younger son of Tex and Dorothy Fay, in the concept of establishing a Tex Ritter Museum in his hometown of Carthage. Tommie learned that the family stored a treasure trove of Tex Ritter memorabilia in a Los Angeles warehouse. The Ritter family agreed to provide this rich collection of materials to a Tex Ritter Museum in Carthage. The primary stipulation of the Ritters was that there would be free admission to the museum for local students and student groups.

In the meantime, two philanthropic Carthage citizens, Pat and Gertrude Patterson, had purchased a historic house two blocks west of the town square. The old Clabaugh home was a rambling, two-story white framed residence with spacious and handsome rooms. The Pattersons donated the building to the city. The chamber of commerce sold the building they were in and put the proceeds into renovating their new headquarters. The chamber moved into the lower floor of the Clabaugh House, while Tommie planned to convert the second story into the Tex Ritter Museum. City of Carthage electricians and carpenters labored to ready the upstairs for its new role as a museum.

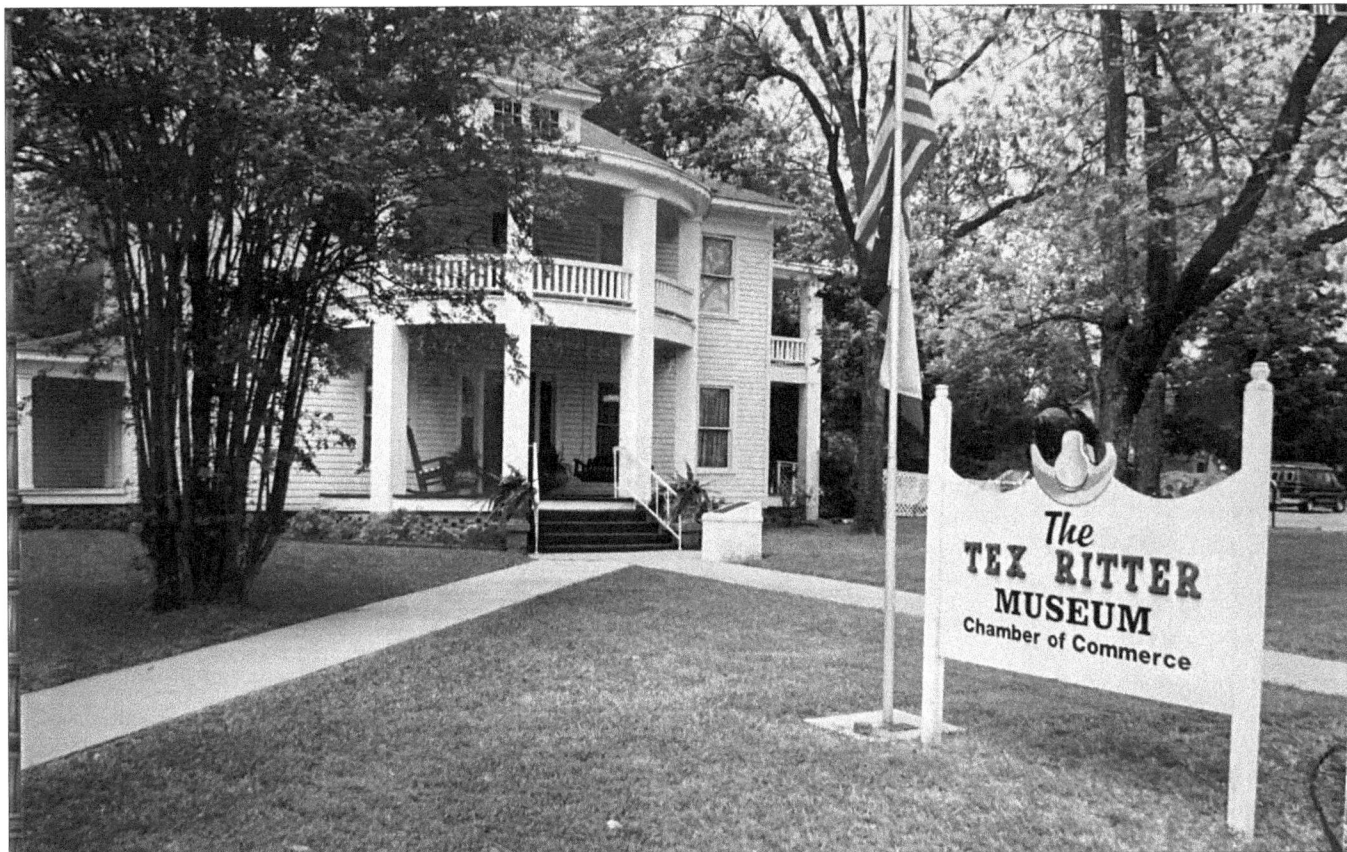

After the spacious Clabaugh House was donated to the City of Carthage, the lower floor became the home of the Panola Chamber of Commerce. The second floor soon housed the Tex Ritter Museum and, beginning in 1998, the Texas Country Music Hall of Fame.

"In 1991," related Tommie, "I made a trip to Los Angeles and was taken to a warehouse completely full of everything that Tex had. There were movie posters, clothes, movies, records, lobby cards, photos, Western folklore books, song collections, awards, etc., everywhere!" Although Tommie brought a few precious artifacts back home on her person, "the Ritters agreed to send the items to Texas for me to establish the Tex Ritter Museum."

When the Tex Ritter memorabilia arrived in Carthage, everything was "unpacked, inventoried, cleaned, framed, and made ready to be exhibited." But Tommie had no experience in assembling museum displays.

"So I made weekend trips to every museum within a day's drive of Carthage to get ideas and take photos of what I liked." Of particular help was Ellie Caston, director of the Gregg County Museum in Longview. Welcome assistance also was provided by the Texas Association of Muse-

ums in Austin.

The Tex Ritter Museum was opened on October 18, 1992. Tommy Ritter, the oldest son of Tex, came from California for the ribbon-cutting; so did nephews Ken and Gordon Ritter, niece Ola Johnson, and their families; Les Leverett, legendary photographer for the *Grand Ole Opry* and WSM in Nashville; and Tex Ritter's close friend and colleague from Nashville, Joe Allison. A large crowd was present for the ceremony, and more than one thousand patrons toured the museum on opening day.

The second floor of the Clabaugh House boasted a profusion of Tex Ritter artifacts and archival files. Nothing anywhere could rival the Tex Ritter collection in Carthage. A steady stream of visitors entered the chamber building and ventured upstairs to visit room after room of Ritter memorabilia.

A great many tourists wanted to purchase a biography of Tex. Tommie Ritter Smith ap-

Carthage City Manager Charles Thomas and Tommie Ritter Smith, with philanthropist Chester Stout in the background, unveil a plaque in front of the Texas Country Music Hall of Fame.

proached Bill O'Neal, a history instructor at Panola College and the author of numerous non-fiction books. Tommie stressed the need for a new book about Tex Ritter, and she generously offered to share the wealth of files, scrapbooks, photos, recordings, and miscellaneous artifacts possessed by the museum. A single phone call to Ed Eakin of Eakin Press produced a book deal. Throughout the project, Tommie provided the author with introductions and phone numbers and responded to every inquiry and request. Tommie Ritter Smith has done more than any other individual to perpetuate the memory and history of Tex Ritter.

Gaylord Enterprises arranged with Tommie to borrow items for a suitable exhibit for Tex Ritter at the Grand Ole Opry Museum. As a result, Tex was the fifth artist inducted into Nashville's Country Music Hall of Fame (in 1964). In addition, he served a highly productive term as the second president of the new organization (Gene Autry was the first president).

Tommie arranged for seventy-five people from Panola County to attend the opening of the Tex Ritter exhibit. Most traveled by chartered bus and enjoyed three days in Nashville. For Bill O'Neal, the trip provided an opportunity to meet and visit with Tex Ritter's sons, Tommy and John. John Ritter took time from a busy evening at the *Grand Ole Opry* to grant a delightful interview backstage. And during the following months, Tommy Ritter tirelessly fielded the author's requests for information and family insights.

In the meantime, a momentous development was taking place. In 1996 Tommie Ritter Smith accepted an invitation to receive an award on behalf of Tex at the induction of Tex Ritter into the East Texas Arts and Entertainment Hall of Fame. At a banquet held in Kilgore, Tommie received a plaque that would be placed in the Tex Ritter Museum.

Rusty Summerville, a museum design specialist with Gaylord Enterprises, made immense contributions to the arrangement of display cases, lighting, and traffic flow of the original TCMHOF museum. As the museum has expanded, Rusty has returned to continue to share his professional expertise.

At this event, Tommie learned that no East Texas Hall of Fame existed, just an organization called the East Texas Arts and Entertainment Council. Before long, this council disbanded, which encouraged Tommie "to investigate the Hall of Fame on our own."

While compiling a list of the many musicians, entertainers, and songwriters from East Texas, it was brought to her to her attention that Panola County was the only county in the entire United States that could boast two members of Nashville's Country Music Hall of Fame: Tex Ritter

and Jim Reeves.

As these ideas were gestating, Tommie was approached by Carthage community leader Chester Stout. Stout was a successful businessman who had participated enthusiastically in local events, and now he wanted to make a substantial donation to honor his late wife, Johnny. Stout was told about the idea of a Hall of Fame addition to the Tex Ritter Museum. Tommie was elated because "he said he would be more than willing to finance this project."

By 1997 local citizens and officials of the City of Carthage and the chamber were enthusiastic about capitalizing on the country music heritage of East Texas.

"We started the paperwork to obtain the charter and IRS exemption immediately." While discussing the matter with the office of the Texas Secretary of State, "it hit me that we didn't need to limit ourselves to East Texas," said Tommie, "so I asked for the name 'Texas Country Music Hall of Fame.'"

Tommie informed City Manager Charles Thomas that the name was available. Like Tommie, Charles was a native of Carthage and served his hometown as city manager for thirty years (1974-2004). Committed to the museum project, Charles arranged for city employees to work on the city-owned museum.

When he heard that the name Texas Country Music Hall of Fame had not been taken, Charles contacted attorney Robert Underwood. Underwood promptly engaged a courier in Austin, and before the day ended, the desired label was assigned to the Carthage institution.

Tommie recalled, "We secured the name, obtained the charter, designed and registered the log, and filed to be a 501(c)(3) organization."

With the Texas Country Music Hall of Fame officially established, an executive board of directors and a museum committee were formed. Tommie consulted with Rusty Summerville, a museum design specialist with Gaylord Enter-

Statue of Gentleman Jim Reeves, located at Jim Reeves Memorial Park adjacent to Highway 79 a few miles east of Carthage.

entire museum was taken down, and displays were removed from the cases for the new construction. Electricians, carpenters, and painters were brought in and started their work. Every room had to be redone."

Simultaneously, board members met to consider the first inductees of the Texas Country Music Hall of Fame. "The criteria was that they must be born in Texas and contributed to the country music profession for a significant number of years." (Later, however, it was recognized that some worthy candidates might have been born in another state but moved to Texas as children with their families.) Reflecting the rich talent pool of Texas country musicians, an initial list of more than 200 eligible prospects was compiled. Board members had the task of narrowing down an impressive group of candidates, and during these sessions, individuals had to make

prises. Since the upstairs of the museum building was full of Tex Ritter exhibits, Rusty advised that the Ritter displays should be moved around to create better traffic flow and, of course, to add display cases for the new hall of fame members. In addition, it was decided that better lighting was required, the rooms should be repainted, and the windows boarded to provide more security and protection from sunlight.

"So," related Tommie, "everything in the

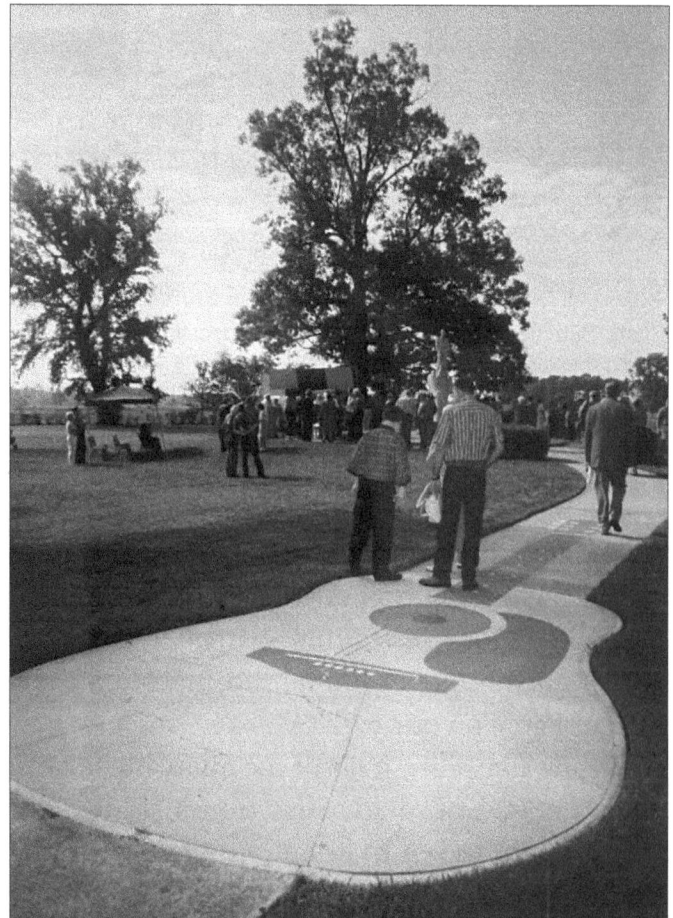

Crowd gathered at Jim Reeves Memorial Park on the opening weekend of the Texas Country Music Hall of Fame.

A trio of country music legends at the opening weekend of the TCMHOF. L to R: famed disc jockey Tom Perryman; Cindy Walker; and emcee Ralph Emery, the "Dick Clark of Country Music."

played guitar throughout her childhood. Also, a gifted songwriter, when Cindy accompanied her father on a business trip to Los Angeles, she boldly marched unannounced into the office of Bing Crosby and pitched her song, "Lone Star Trail," which Crosby recorded.

Signed to a Decca contract, soon Cindy entered a collaboration with Bob Wills, composing fifty songs for the Texas Playboys. She also wrote hit songs for Gene Autry, Jim Reeves, Er-

the case for various distinguished artists.

The six charter inductees were: Tex Ritter, Jim Reeves, Gene Autry, Willie Nelson, Cindy Walker, and Joe Allison. Ritter and Reeves were deceased, but John and Tommy Ritter committed to attend and receive their father's plaque. The sisters of Jim Reeves, along with their families, also planned to attend. Gene Autry was suffering health difficulties and was unable to travel. Tommie Ritter Smith and some board members flew to Los Angeles to present his TCMHOF plaque at his 90th birthday party. But the "Singing Cowboy" superstar was well represented at the Carthage ceremony, although he passed away only a few weeks after the first TCMHOF induction.

Cindy Walker, living in her hometown of Mexia, Texas, was eager to participate in the induction. She invited Tommie Ritter Smith and her husband Bill to lunch, a formal affair served by Cindy's housekeeper. Afterward, Cindy showed Tommie and Bill her memorabilia, some of which would be displayed at the TCMHOF. Tommie learned that when Willie Nelson was in the vicinity, his tour bus would turn down the narrow street and stop at Cindy's home. Other performers' busses also would navigate the little street for visits with Cindy Walker.

A born performer, Cindy sang, danced, and

Cindy Walker, wearing the dress her mother had lovingly given her, advances to receive her Hall of Fame plaque. Cindy was inspired to write a poem for the occasion.

Les Leverett, official photographer of the *Grand Ole Opry*, attended the TCMHOF weekend every year to visit his friends and, inevitably, to shoot photos. Les donated one of his cameras, along with other artifacts from his notable career, to the TCMHOF museum.

nest Tubb, Glen Campbell, Ricky Skaggs, Webb Pierce, and many other artists.

Known as "the greatest living songwriter of country music," Cindy became a charter inductee of the Nashville Songwriters Hall of Fame in 1970. In addition, she was voted into the Country Music Association Hall of Fame. Following her induction into the TCMHOF, Cindy composed a song in honor of the "Texas Hall of Fame," and she attended subsequent ceremonies until her death in 2006.

Joe Allison was a close friend and associate of Tex Ritter. A native of McKinney, Texas, Joe became a popular radio announcer, working behind microphones in Nashville, Memphis, and Los Angeles. Joe was elected to both the DJ Hall of Fame and the Nashville Songwriters Hall of

Fame, writing a number of hit songs and producing records for numerous artists. Joe also toured with Tex Ritter's traveling show and appeared on television with Tex in the syndicated *Town Hall Party*. Like Cindy Walker, Joe Allison eagerly participated in TCMHOF annual activities.

Willie Nelson brought enormous star power to the inaugural ceremony of the Texas Country Music Hall of Fame. Already a musical legend and a movie star, Willie cheerfully agreed to perform at the first induction, even though he and his band had to travel back to Texas from Colorado. On induction weekend Willie's tour bus drove all night, then highballed into Carthage in time for the show. And when Willie stepped off the bus, he was nattily attired for the occasion in a distinctive tuxedo.

Another prominent member of the country music world served as emcee for the induction ceremony. Ralph Emery, known as the "Dick Clark of Country Music," starred for more than half a century over the most powerful broadcast outlets in country music. During 1965 and 1966, Tex Ritter co-starred on Emery's *Opry Star Spotlight*, an all-night show over Nashville's WSM Radio. So when asked by Tommie Ritter Smith to be master of ceremonies for the first induction of the Texas Country Music Hall of Fame, Emery immediately agreed "to do that for Tex." Ralph Emery returned to Carthage year after year to helm the show, and with limitless contacts in country music, he was invaluable assistance in arranging performances for the TCMHOF.

The date for the ribbon-cutting of the Texas Country Music Hall of Fame show was set for Saturday, August 22, 1998. The TCMHOF would welcome guests following an eleven o'clock ribbon-cutting on August 22, while the evening induction program would be staged at the largest auditorium in Carthage. A state-of-the-art high school was erected in Carthage in 1949, boasting, among other features, a 1,100-seat audito-

Tommie Ritter Smith provided a television interview on the lawn of the Texas Country Music Hall of Fame during the 1998 Grand Opening, which attracted widespread media coverage.

rium. There were 850 seats downstairs and 250 seats in the balcony. When a more modern high school opened in 1981, the former CHS building became a junior high, but the 1949 auditorium remained the largest venue in town.

At last, detailed preparations could be made, and the Tex Ritter Museum — now the Texas Country Music Hall of Fame — could be pieced together. But, at this crucial stage, disaster struck.

On July 4, 1998, seven weeks before the opening of the new museum and the TCMHOF induction, Tommie and Bill Smith were involved in a near-fatal automobile crash. While returning to Carthage from a birthday celebration for Bill's father in Haynesville, La., the Smith auto hydroplaned and slid into the oncoming lane of traffic.

Bill was treated for broken ribs and a severe leg injury. Tommie was air flighted to a Shreveport hospital, where it was learned that she had suffered a concussion and dental injuries, and her pelvis was broken in six places.

"I remained in the hospital for two weeks," reminisced Tommie ruefully. "Needless to say, I was in a panic because everything in the museum was on the floor, and our opening was just weeks away."

Tommie returned to work in a wheelchair. "Thanks to my husband and many volunteers who worked late into the night, brought food, and even took me to therapy at the local hospital, we made the deadline and opened the museum as scheduled." Compounding Tommie's personal difficulties: "I buried my mother on August 10 of that year."

With the promise of a Willie Nelson performance, with honorees including Gene Autry, Tex Ritter, Jim Reeves, Cindy Walker, and the popular Joe Allison, and a star-studded country show conducted by Ralph Emery, fans and country music performers turned out in great numbers.

Members of the country music world were there to see and be seen.

One hour before noon on Saturday, August 22, a large crowd gathered on the lawn of the old Clabaugh House — now the new Texas Country Music Hall of Fame. There were television and radio interviews. Lined up just behind the ribbon were inductee Joe Allison, local philanthropist Chester Stout (armed with a large pair of ceremonial scissors), TCMHOF Director Tommie Ritter Smith, and Tom Ritter, son of Tex.

After the ribbon was cut, excited crowds flocked through the museum rooms while many out-of-towners drove for a visit to the Jim Reeves Memorial Park and statue. Word continued to trickle in by phone about the progress of Willie Nelson's bus, which arrived with little time to spare and parked just behind the backstage entrance.

One of many pleasurable activities of the day was the publication release of *Tex Ritter, America's Most Beloved Cowboy*. The Ritter biography was illustrated with more than 200 photos, all beautifully displayed on glossy pages. Representatives of Eakin Press were available throughout the day to provide copies. That evening, during the lengthy intermission, the author sat at a table between John and Tom Ritter, who each provided autographs for book purchasers.

The auditorium was a sellout for the star-studded induction ceremony: fifty dollars per seat downstairs and twenty-five dollars for balcony seating. Many attendees came in formal evening wear, or at least country western dress clothing. Ralph Emery was smooth and polished, announcing performers with lively humor and presenting the impressive Hall of Fame plaques with dignity and style. Lovely Jan Howard voiced Tex Ritter songs. Artists sang and played with talent and excitement, and the highlight of the evening was Willie Nelson's performance. Afterward, Willie signed autographs and provided an impromptu concert outside his bus

until two in the morning. Carthage fell in love with Willie, and Nelson, in turn, was delighted with Carthage.

Willie would be back. And so would Ralph Emery and Joe Allison, Cindy Walker and Tom Ritter, and a parade of popular country performers. Indeed, visitors from Nashville renewed their hotel reservations for the next year before departing for home. Many members of the 1998 audience also returned, year after year. And when larger venues were later developed in Carthage, the groups of regular attendees expanded to even more faithful audience members eager to see superb and memorable live entertainment in the Piney Woods of East Texas. The

Carthage Mayor Carson Joines offering a welcome to the Grand Opening crowd.

A significant element of the development of the TCMHOF was a large statue of Tex Ritter. Small versions were sold to raise funding, and Ritter's two sons, as well as his close friends, Joe and Rita Allison, examined one of the statuettes. From left to right are Tom Ritter, Joe Allison, Rita Allison, and popular television star John Ritter.

An hour before noon on Saturday, August 22, 1998, an enthusiastic crowd gathered for the ribbon-cutting ceremony of the Texas Country Music Hall of Fame. Holding the ribbon and scissors at the Grand Opening are, from left to right in the front row: Joe Allison, a member of the Nashville Songwriters Hall of Fame; Chester Stout of Carthage, whose philanthropy was instrumental in developing the museum; Tommie Ritter Smith, director of the TCMHOF; Tom Ritter, oldest son of Tex Ritter; and, at far right, sculptor Bob Harness.

John and Tom Ritter with sculptor Bob Harness.

John and Tom Ritter holding the Hall of Fame plaque honoring their father. Joining the Ritters is lovely Jan Howard, who sang the hits of Tex Ritter.

The Tex Ritter statue in its first — and temporary — location.

Legendary Country singer Kitty Wells – a spectacular guest performer at the first TCMHOF induction – is flanked by her son, Bobby Wright, and husband, Johnny Wright.

Willie Nelson highballed from an out-of-state engagement into Carthage in his tour bus. Arriving in time for the inaugural indication ceremony, his performance was the highlight of the evening. Afterwards, Willie signed autographs and provided an impromptu concert until two in the morning.

Willie Nelson with his Hall of Fame plaque.

Chapter Four

More Stars and a New Hall of Fame Building

During the first Hall of Fame celebration, Tommie Ritter Smith spent induction evening in a wheelchair because of her recent automobile accident. So instead of being busily involved backstage, she was seated in the audience.

During the star-studded performances, Tommie began to recall her high school appearances on this same stage. On this memorable evening, she was surrounded by a standing-room-only crowd exceeding 1,100. Onstage throughout the night were such beloved celebrities as Kitty Wells, Willie Nelson, John Ritter, and Cindy Walker. Frances Preston, the CEO of BMI (Broadcast Music, Inc.), was part of the program, and so was Bill Whitaker, head of the *Grand Ole Opry*.

Tommie suddenly realized that these eminent people had come to her hometown, that this notable event was taking place at her former high school, because of the unexpected path of her employment with the chamber of commerce, the subsequent creation of the Tex Ritter Museum, and the development of the Texas Country Music Hall of Fame — which brought Nashville to Carthage, Texas, for the thrilling opening of this important new institution. For a moment, Tommie was overwhelmed with emotion and the determination to redouble her efforts to continue the expansion of the Texas Country Music Hall of Fame and its activities.

Following the success of the opening of the Texas Country Music Hall of Fame, board members and Carthage community leaders excitedly began to plan for the 1999 induction weekend. With six illustrious country stars inducted in 1998 to start the museum, four more standout artists in 1999 would bring the Hall of Fame membership to a respectable total of ten. And

it proved easy to determine four additional legendary Country luminaries for 1999: Ernest Tubb, Hank Thompson, Waylon Jennings, and Bill Mack.

Ernest Tubb was known as "ET" and "The Texas Troubadour." His twangy, gravelly singing voice proved popular, and he good-naturedly agreed with fans who said they could sing better.

"I don't care whether I hit the right note or not," he laughed. "I don't read music, and I'd fight the man who tried to teach me. I'm not looking for perfection of delivery — thousands of singers have that. I'm looking for individuality. I phrase the way I want to: I sing the way I feel like singing at the moment."

In 1941 ET enjoyed an enormous hit that he composed and recorded, "Walkin' the Floor Over You," which eventually sold over one million copies. He sang his hit in a Charles Starrett movie, then appeared in another Starrett film. And he used his growing popularity to help shift the emphasis of country and western from hillbilly to western.

ET moved to Nashville in 1943 as a member of the *Grand Ole Opry*. He became the first entertainer to use an electric guitar on the *Opry*. In 1947 ET opened the Ernest Tubb Record Shop around the corner from the Ryman Auditorium. The *Midnight Jamboree* radio show's live broadcast emanated from ET's record shop after each Saturday night *Opry* show. Also, in 1947, ET became the first country artist to play New York's Carnegie Hall.

ET and his band, the Texas Troubadours, recorded one hit after another. Of fifty-four singles they recorded in the fifteen years after 1944, only four failed to crack the top ten, and these four made the top fifteen. ET's favorite song, "Waltz Across Texas," was recorded in 1964. The Texas Troubadour was elected to the CMA Hall of Fame in 1965, and later, he was inducted into the CMA and the Nashville Songwriters Hall of Fame.

Even after contracting emphysema, ET continued to make over 200 appearances a year, carrying an oxygen tank on his bus. After each performance, the Texas Troubadour was the last person to leave the auditorium, shaking hands and signing autographs with every fan who wanted to stay. Unfortunately, health problems finally halted his performances in 1982, and he died two years later.

ET was represented at the 1999 TCMHOF induction by Merle Kilgore, a fellow member of the Nashville Songwriters Hall of Fame and a Texas Country Music Hall of Fame board member. In addition to Merle Kilgore, numerous other stars enhanced the 1999 show, including beautiful Connie Smith and Rex Allen, Jr., son of Hollywood's last "Singing Cowboy."

Waylon Jennings was a 1999 inductee who, as a young artist, played bass with Buddy Holly. "Mainly, what I learned from Buddy was an attitude," reminisced Waylon. "He loved music, and he taught me that it shouldn't have any barriers to it."

Despite the success Waylon soon enjoyed in Nashville, by the 1970s, he felt confined by the string-laden and pop-oriented Nashville sound. "Every business has a system that works for eighty percent of the people who are in it," explained Waylon, "but there's always that other twenty percent who just don't fit in. That's what happened to me, and it happened to Willie Nelson. We just couldn't do it the way it was set up. It wasn't until I started producing my own records and using my own musicians and working with people who understand what I was about that I first started having any real success."

In 1999 Merle Kilgore, popular Country artist and industry executive, accepted the Hall of Fame plaque for Ernest Tubb. Tubb, "The Texas Troubadour," was a longtime star of the *Grand Ole Opry* and a member of Nashville's Country Music Hall of Fame.

Waylon's success was explosive. Recording with his own band and producing his own records, he moved outside the Nashville sound to "outlaw music," His powerful voice and personality put a strong stamp on country music, which owes much of its broad appeal and rugged individualism to the artist often called "Hoss."

Through the years, Waylon enjoyed thirteen gold albums. *Ol' Waylon*, released in 1977, became the first country album by a solo artist to go platinum. Two years later, his *Greatest Hits* entered new territory by going quadruple platinum. Waylon has sold more than 40 million records worldwide. He followed his vision and became a giant of country music.

Unfortunately, by the 1990s, Waylon had developed serious health problems triggered by cocaine addiction, chain-smoking, and diabetes. He had open-heart surgery in 1988, and his left foot was amputated late in life. Waylon Jennings died in 2002 of diabetic complications.

Therefore, when Tommie Ritter Smith notified Waylon of his 1999 nomination to the Texas Country Music Hall of Fame, he was already finding it difficult to travel and was cutting back on most of his concert appearances. Although Waylon confidently signed the TCMHOF contract requiring him to appear at the induction ceremony, he began to express doubts as August 1999 approached. Tommie Ritter Smith offered to provide transportation by private bus or plane, but Waylon recognized that he was physically unable to make the journey to Carthage. Although the TCMHOF audience was disappointed, Tommie Ritter Smith later traveled to Nashville to deliver Waylon's plaque in person.

Bill Mack, "The Midnight Cowboy," invited Connie Smith to sing a selection of his hits at his 1999 induction.

Bill Mack, "The Midnight Cowboy," was the number one disc jockey in Texas and was known throughout the nation as the dean of country music disc jockeys. In addition, he was a country performer and producer, as well as an accomplished songwriter.

Bill Mack was born in 1929 in Shamrock, Texas. As a singer and songwriter, he performed Texas rockabilly and recorded for several labels. His country broadcasting career began in the late 1940s. Bill served as an announcer for Bob Wills on radio and television for ten years.

For more than four decades, he hosted the all-night *Bill Mack Trucking Show* over WBAP-AM out of Dallas-Fort Worth. Beamed throughout the USA, Canada, and Mexico via the Bill Mack Trucking Network, the midnight to 5 a.m. show featured trucker call-ins and a wide variety of guests. Bill also hosted *Country Crossroads*, heard every weekend on more than 1,000 stations across the nation.

The Midnight Cowboy was recognized as the number disc jockey in Texas for more than twenty-five years, and in 1982 he was inducted into the Country Music Hall of Fame in Nashville.

Songs written by Bill were recorded by Dean Martin, George Strait, Jerry Lee Lewis, Ray Price, Connie Smith, Conway Twitty, and dozens of other artists. In the Dallas area, Bill Mack discovered a little girl with a powerhouse voice. LeAnn Rimes was an only child who had been given vocal and dramatic training. At this point, Bill directed her career, and in 1996, after she had performed more than 100 concerts and made numerous television appearances, thirteen-year-old LeAnn recorded a song Mack had written in the 1950s. "Blue" was a sensation for LeAnn Rimes, breaking sales records. "Blue" was named Country Song of the Year, and Bill Mack received a cherished Grammy as a composer. Bill termed the Grammy "an unbelievable thrill." Bill asked Connie Smith to perform his greatest hits at the TCMHOF, and the lovely star

Rex Allen, Jr., son of Hollywood's last singing cowboy, performed throughout the weekend of the 1999 induction. The popular television and recording star delighted audiences for two days.

was a popular addition to the show.

The climax of the 1999 TCMHOF celebration was a thirty-minute performance by Hank Thompson and his standout band, the Brazos Valley Boys. A native of Waco, Hank won talent contests as a boy and learned to play a four-dollar guitar after seeing a Gene Autry movie. As a teenager, he performed on local radio as "Hank the Hired Hand."

After graduating from high school in 1943, Hank enlisted in the Navy and served as a radio operator in the Pacific. Hank brought his guitar aboard ship and performed when off duty.

"A lot of people heard Hank Thompson for the first time on ships," he laughed. "They didn't have much choice unless they wanted to jump overboard."

After the war, Hank landed a noontime radio show back in Waco, then organized a band. As a result of his electronics experience in the Navy, Hank and the Brazos Valley Boys were the first music act to tour with a sound and lighting system.

Hank was the first country music artist to play Las Vegas, and his *Live at the Golden Nugget* was the first "live" country album ever recorded. When Hank turned to television, *The Hank Thompson Show* was the first telecast of a variety show.

Hank charted hits in five different decades, including "The Wild Side of Life," "Rub-a-Dub," "Smokey, the Bear," "The Older the Violin the Sweeter the Music," and "A Six Pack to Go." Hank's sales would top sixty million records. He was a 1989 inductee into Nashville's Country Music Hall of Fame and, in 1997, the Songwriters Hall of Fame. Hank passed away in 2007 at the age of eighty-two, performing until the very end of his life.

A major event of the 2000 induction ceremony was unveiling a magnificent statue of Tex Ritter and his stallion, White Flash. For many years country music fans — from Texas, other states, and other nations — had trekked to Panola County to see the statue of Gentleman Jim Reeves. Following the tragic death of Reeves in 1964, his widow hastily arranged to have the Panola County native interred a few miles east of

Hank Thompson and his award-winning band, the Brazos Valley Boys, performed a crowd-pleasing half-hour set prior to his 1999 induction.

A highlight of 1999 was the performance of the famed Kilgore Rangerettes.

Carthage beside Highway 79.

A two-acre plot was acquired by Carthage attorneys Tom Bankhead and Tommy George Davis, and following the burial service, a lovely memorial park was developed. The park features a tall statue of Gentleman Jim, and as country music fans flocked to see the TCMHOF, a great many visited the Reeves statue and park. Indeed, on the morning of the first induction ceremony, a large crowd witnessed the dedication of a Texas Historical Marker at the Reeves park and statue. It soon became clear that a statue of Tex Ritter should be erected at the Texas Country Music Hall of Fame.

Fortunately, a talented sculptor had recently moved to Carthage. Bob Harness was a former marine who spent more than thirty years as a commercial artist in Kansas City. Harness and his wife moved to Carthage in 1995. After Tommie Ritter Smith viewed Bob's small bronze statues, a commission was arranged for the museum's larger-than-life statue of Tex Ritter.

Harness worked for three years to create a bronze statue of Tex and White Flash. The sculptor envisioned Tex seated on a large rock strumming a guitar and singing a tune while a saddled White Flash stood just behind. Harness studied and measured photographs to produce a meticulously detailed image. The sitting figure of Tex measures seven and a half feet to the crown of his hat, while White Flash is eight feet tall at the shoulders.

The clay form required almost one thousand hours to produce, as Harness worked about forty hours each week for several months. Harness was aided by the Panola College welding and art departments, along with many individual volunteers. Finally, the creation was dismantled and transported to the Dallas Fine Arts Foundry. Tommie Ritter Smith and Charles Thomas led a delegation from Carthage to observe this crucial and interesting part of the process. When the statue was returned to Carthage, Harness applied fi-

nal touches. The completed work weighed close to 3,000 pounds.

The bronze statue was placed on a temporary mount on the lawn just east of the proposed TCMHOF building. The unveiling took place at 9:30 a.m. on Saturday, August 19, 2000. It was a spectacular beginning to the third induction day of the TCMHOF, and an expectant crowd applauded and cheered as the cover was lifted. Two years later, the impressive statue was moved about one hundred yards to the west in front of the entrance to the new TCMHOF building.

With ten stars already installed in the TCMHOF, display space was becoming tight on the second floor above the chamber of commerce building. Plans were in progress to construct a larger, modern facility to house the Texas Country Music Hall of Fame, but for 2000 it was decided to induct just three new members: Dale Evans, Bob Wills, and Charles Walker.

* * * *

Dale Evans, a lovely and talented Texas singer-actress, established herself in the 1940s as Hollywood's most renowned western leading lady. Co-starring with Roy Rogers, the phenomenally popular "King of the Cowboys," Dale earned international fame as the "Queen of the West."

When Frances Octavia Smith was a child, she dreamed of marrying western movie star Tom Mix. "We would have six children together," she reminisced, "then gallop our horses through the sagebrush. . ." She had the script right, but she would have to cast a different cowboy star as her leading man.

She was born in Uvalde, Texas, on October 31, 1912. Her father was a cotton farmer, and she also spent considerable time at her grandparents' rural home in Italy, south of Fort Worth.

Frances loved to sing, dance, and play the piano, and she dreamed of becoming an actress. But after the Smith family moved to a farm in Arkansas, young Frances impulsively married

With Dale Evans unable to travel to Texas, three of her granddaughters dubbed themselves the "Rogers Legacy" and journeyed to Carthage. The trio performed Dale's songs and accepted her plaque.

mail poured in praising his lovely new leading lady. Dale would co-star in twenty-eight Roy Rogers movies, and in 1947 she made the first of four appearances on thet top ten list of money-making cowboy stars. Roy reigned as number one for twelve years, and in the nineteen years that this list existed, Dale was the only female ever named to the top ten.

In 1946 Roy's wife died after giving birth to their third child. Roy and Dale married on the last day of 1947 and eventually added four more children — three by adoption — to their large family. Sadly, three of their nine children died by illness or accident. Nevertheless, Roy and Dale increasingly relied upon their Christian beliefs, and Dale became an important inspirational author and speaker.

another teenager. Although she later gave birth to a son, Tom, her marriage soon ended. The single mother returned to her parents, who had moved to Memphis. Frances took a secretarial job with an insurance company.

Overhearing Frances singing at work, her boss arranged for her to perform on a company-sponsored Memphis radio show. Her talents brought her rapid success as a radio singer, and soon she was hired in larger markets in Dallas and Chicago. At KHAS in Louisville, the station manager changed her name to Dale Evans.

Beckoned to Hollywood, she took screen tests and was featured on a number of network radio programs. After the outbreak of World War II, Dale recorded for overseas broadcasts and performed more than 500 USO shows at army and navy bases in California and surrounding states.

Dale began appearing in musicals and melodramas at Republic Studios, along with a John Wayne. In 1944 she was assigned to a Roy Rogers film, *Cowboy and the Samaritan*. Roy and Dale had obvious on-screen chemistry, and fan

From 1951 through 1956, Roy and Dale co-starred in a popular television series, *The Roy Rogers Show*, and her most famous composition, "Happy Trails," became the show's theme song. In addition, they hosted a variety hour, *The Roy Rogers and Dale Evans Show*, in 1962 and made numerous guest appearances on other shows.

After more than fifty years of marriage, Roy died in 1998 at the age of eighty-six. Despite her own health problems, Dale continued to appear on religious programs. But by 2000, when she was approaching eighty-eight, Dale was suffering from congestive heart failure. Dale intended to fly from California to Texas, but her physician flatly forbade such a trip. Dale, however, was ably represented in Carthage by three of her granddaughters, who performed with great enthusiasm and ability. A few months later, in Feb-

When Bob Wills was inducted posthumously into the TCMHOF in 2000, veteran musicians formed a Texas Playboys reunion band, with Leon Rausch (second from left) as lead singer. Rausch would return as an inductee in 2018.

ruary 2011, Dale Evans passed away.

* * * *

Bob Wills, who died in 1975, was represented at the TCMHOF by his famous band, the Texas Playboys. The western swing band continued to perform for more than a decade following Bob's death. After that, the Playboys reunited for special occasions. The Hall of Fame induction of Bob Wills was one of those occasions, and the talented veterans splendidly entertained the Carthage audience. At one point, Cindy Walker stepped onstage to dance with singer Leon Rausch.

As described in chapter two, Bob Wills arrived in Fort Worth from the Texas Panhandle during the late 1920s, a gifted and innovative fiddler who was instrumental in developing western swing. During the big band era, Bob built the Texas Playboys into the largest band in

country music, heading his group with exuberant dance steps and "Ah Hahs" as he fiddled. Bob Wills and his Texas Playboys performed in a dozen western movies and entertained fans in countless personal appearances and on radio airwaves.

* * * *

During a long and varied career, Charlie Walker was a recording star, noted deejay, championship golfer, golfing broadcaster, and a Las Vegas emcee. As a young serviceman, Charlie even introduced country music to Japan.

Charlie Walker's country roots were authentic. Born in 1926, he was brought up on a Collin County cotton farm near Nevada, north of Dallas. Encouraged by his father to pursue a musical career, Charlie sang and played guitar. At the age of seventeen in 1943, he took a deejay job with KIOX Radio in Bay City, Texas.

With World War II still raging the next year, eighteen-year-old Charlie Walker entered the US Army. Stationed in Japan with occupation forces, Charlie organized a hillbilly band with talented Eighth Army musicians. For the first time, Japanese airwaves carried the sounds of live country music over the American Radio Forces Network.

Following his discharge, Charlie resumed his deejay career with KMAC Radio in San Antonio. His deep understanding of music led him to be listed for ten years by *Billboard* as one of the top ten country deejays in the United States.

But he continued to perform, and after signing a contract with Columbia Records, Charlie

Charlie Walker, 2000 inductee, entertains the crowd before being presented his Hall of Fame plaque.

responded with his biggest hit, "Pick Me Up On Your Way Down." From 1956 through 1966, twenty-five Charlie Walker tunes reached the country charts, and a series of albums followed.

Charlie became a popular member of the *Grand Ole Opry* in 1967. His Las Vegas performances were so well-received that the Golden Nugget engaged him as an emcee-performer for twenty-five weeks a year during the mid-1960s.

An avid golfer, he regularly finished near the leaders in the Las Vegas Sahara International, and in 1966 Charlie won Nashville's Music City Pro-Celebrity Tournament. Also, during the 1960s, he provided television commentary on the Texas Open Golf Tournament for CBS.

With a friendly and easy-going temperament, Charlie was a favorite of his fellow performers and a crowd-pleaser, whether the crowd was radio listeners, a golf gallery, or a Las Vegas audience. Certainly, the 2000 TCMHOF audience was greatly entertained by Charlie Walker. And like a number of inductees, Charlie would happily return as a guest performer at future TCMHOF celebrations.

By 2001 a large sign announced the pending construction of the Texas Country Music Hall of Fame building, but it would be the next year before the museum would open in its modern and expanded quarters. And for the foreseeable future, the induction ceremonies would continue to be held in their original venue under the masterful direction of Ralph Emery.

* * * *

The 2001 inductees would be Ray Price, "The Cherokee Cowboy"; Billy Walker, "The Tall Texan"; and Stuart Hamblin, "Radio's First Singing Cowboy."

"Make the World Go Away." "Release Me." "For the Good Times." "Crazy Arms." "Burning Memories." "Heartaches By the Number." From 1952 through 1982, the velvet voice of Ray Price recorded more than eighty hits that soared into the country music top forty, along with numer-

The velvet voice of Ray Price propelled more than eighty songs into the country music Top 40. Dubbed the "Cherokee Cowboy," Price became a member of the *Grand Ole Opry* in 1952, Nashville's Country Music Hall of Fame in 1996, and the Texas Country Music Hall of Fame in 2001.

ous crossover hits. In addition, the memorable artistry of Ray Price has included notable innovations. So when he was voted into the Country Music Hall of Fame in 1996, there was a widespread feeling that the honor was long overdue.

Ray Noble Price was born in East Texas, at little Perryville, southeast of Winnsboro, on January 12, 1926. (January 12 also was Tex Ritter's birth date.) When he was four, his parents divorced, and his mother moved with little Ray to Dallas. When Ray graduated from Adamson High School in Dallas, World War II was raging. The eighteen-year-old enlisted in the U.S. Marines in 1944, serving in the Pacific. Discharged in 1946, he enrolled in a Dallas-area college, intending to become a veterinarian.

But his musical talents led to college gigs and other local dates. By 1948, billing himself as "The Cherokee Kid" (soon changed to "The Cherokee Cowboy"), Ray joined Abilene's *Hillbilly Jamboree*, broadcast over KRBC Radio. The next year he moved to the *Big D Jamboree*, which was nationally telecast over Dallas' CBS affiliate. Ray made his first recordings over the Dallas-based Bullet label, but he signed with Columbia in 1951.

By this time, he had become close friends with his idol, Hank Williams, who wrote a song, "Weary Blues," for Ray. This connection with Hank Williams was instrumental in Ray's invitation to join the *Grand Ole Opry* in 1952, the year his recordings began to reach the charts.

After Hank's death early in 1953, his Drifting Cowboys became Ray's backup band, and the young artist patterned himself stylistically after Williams. But one night, an audience member told him, "Ray, you sound more like ol' Hank every time I hear you."

Ray realized he needed to find his own sound, and the rest of his career would be a musical adventure. So, dismissing the Drifting Cowboys, he formed a new band, the Cherokee Cowboys. Notable artists who, at one time or another, were members of the Cherokee Cowboys included Willie Nelson, Roger Miller, and Johnny Paycheck.

Within a year, Ray added a drum set to the Cherokee Cowboys. Although Bob Wills used drums with his famous dance band, country bands of the era did not include drums, "and certainly not on the *Grand Ole Opry*," recalled Price. But by introducing drums, the Cherokee Cowboys were able to emphasize the "Ray Price

Beat," a distinctive shuffle beat that quickly spread throughout country music.

"It lends itself to a kind of a dance motion for the song," analyzed Ray. "You have to sing a song slow enough to get the emotion and everything in it that you need, but you don't want it so slow it sounds like a funeral march. The shuffle is just a way of making it sound like it's going faster than it is."

Country music fans thought Ray Price and his band were becoming rockabilly like Elvis and Carl Perkins. But in 1956, Ray's "Crazy Arms" spent forty-five weeks on the country charts, including twenty weeks as number one. As he reeled off one hit after another, the "Ray Price Beat" became a standard country sound.

By the 1960s, Ray began slipping strings into such country hits as "Make the World Go Away" (1963) and "Burning Memories" (1964). In 1967 he was backed by forty-seven pieces when he recorded "Danny Boy." Although some country deejays boycotted him, "Danny Boy" broke into the top ten. In 1970 there were more strings when Ray covered Kris Kristofferson's "For the Good Times," which reached number one and also hit the pop charts.

"I've always ricocheted from one side to the other," explained Ray. "If you're going to have a record, you've got to overcome the last hit you've had. The only way I think you can do that is come out of left field somewhere with something they just don't expect."

Although in his mid-seventies, when he was inducted into the TCMHOF, this innovative stylist continued to leave his East Texas ranch and wife of three decades to record and perform 100 dates per year. "Times are changing. People want to hear music." But, as Ray Price contemplated his future musical possibilities, he warned, "They'd better watch this old man."

* * * *

In 1942, thirteen-year-old farm boy Billy Walker picked more than 320 pounds of cotton

Raised on cotton farms in West Texas, Billy Walker grew to six-three and became known as "The Tall Texan." Inspired during boyhood by a Gene Autry movie, Billy saved up for a guitar and eventually scored thirty-four top ten hits. He opened for Hank Thompson, joined the Louisiana Hayride, and later became a popular member of the *Grand Ole Opry*.

in one grueling day. Then, rewarded by his father with a quarter, Billy treated himself to a Gene Autry movie, *Cowboy Serenade*.

"That's what hooked me on show business," reminisced Billy half a century later. "That's where I wanted to be."

Show business offered an escape from a difficult upbringing. Billy Marvin Walker was born on a West Texas farm near Ralls on January 14, 1929. Billy was one of eight children, but when he was four, his mother died while trying to give birth to a ninth baby. It was the heart of the Great Depression, and Billy's father was forced to place his three youngest children — Jerry, Billy, and Delmar — in a Methodist orphanage in Waco. Billy hated life in an orphanage dormitory. "It was like being in prison."

After a few years, the family was reunited, but life on a West Texas cotton farm was hard. "I made spending money by plucking turkeys for between three and eight cents a bird," he recalled. After seeing *Cowboy Serenade*, Billy saved enough money to buy a guitar for $3.25 and an instruction book for another quarter. "From then on, I practiced and worked on songs every spare minute."

When he was fifteen, Billy won a talent competition in Ralls. He was awarded three dollars, a chocolate cake, and a fifteen-minute show on Saturday mornings at a New Mexico radio station. There was no pay, only exposure, and experience, but Billy eagerly hitch-hiked eighty miles each way on Saturdays.

After high school, Billy advanced quickly, soon forming his own trio. "When I was nineteen," he related, "Hank Thompson hired me as his opening act, which led to a Capitol Records recording contract."

Billing himself as "The Traveling Texan," he joined the *Big D Jamboree* from KRLD Radio in Dallas. Topping out at six-foot-three, he would also be known as "The Tall Texan," Eventually, Billy would develop a Tall Texan record label.

From 1952 through 1955, he was a member of Shreveport's prestigious *Louisiana Hayride*, touring with such *Hayride* stars as Hank Williams, Webb Pierce, and Faron Young. Indeed, Billy was part of the last tour with Williams before Hank died, and he was present when young Elvis Presley debuted with the Hayride.

Billy first hit made the charts in 1954, and he enjoyed thirty-four top ten Hits through the years. In 1962 his single "Charlie's Shoes" reached number one and stayed on the charts for five months. *Billboard* voted him as one of the top twenty most played artists from 1950-1970.

In 1960 Billy became a member of the *Grand Ole Opry*, remaining one of its most loyal participants. Three years later, Billy and Hawkshaw Hawkins traded flights because of a family emergency. Billy flew safely to Nashville, but a few hours later, the small plane carrying Hawkshaw, Cowboy Copas, and Patsy Cline crashed, killing all aboard.

"Ever since then, I have felt that God did not let me on that plane," reflected Billy. "He had other things in mind for me."

In the 1970s, Billy, backed by his group, the Tennessee Walkers, headlined his own television show, *Country Music Carousel*. In addition, he appeared on the *Jimmy Dean Show*, *The Statler Brothers Show*, *Hee Haw*, and many other televi-

"Tugboat Jerry" cheerfully served as a guest performer during several of the early induction weekends.

sion shows. The Traveling Texan played almost every state fair and major arena in the United States and toured throughout Europe and Asia. His gentlemanly deportment won him widespread popularity and friendships.

Billy was the father of six daughters. Although his first two marriages ended in divorce, he found lasting happiness in a 1978 marriage. Bettie Walker operated Billy Walker Enterprises from their suburban home near Nashville, and Billy remained a popular ambassador for country music.

Tragically, Billy and Bettie were killed in 2006 while returning to Nashville from a performance in Alabama. The van Billy was driving veered off the Interstate and overturned. Two band members also died, but Billy's grandson, Joshua Brooks, survived his injuries.

* * * *

"When you see me fall asleep, say amen but don't you weep. I've got so many million years that I can't count them."

This expression of deep religious belief came from an East Texas preacher's son. As a Hollywood performer, he strayed far from his boyhood faith, then returned to God as a religious composer of great power and popularity.

Carl Stuart Hamblen was born at Kellyville, west of Jefferson, Texas, on October 20, 1908. His father was an itinerant preacher, and Stuart learned to love outdoor life while traveling with him. Enrolling at a Methodist institution in Abilene, McMurry College, Stuart soon became a singing cowboy on KAYO Radio in Abilene. In 1929, he won a talent contest in Dallas three years later.

With his $100 cash prize, Stuart traveled to the east coast, recording four songs for the forerunner of RCA Victor. Then he ventured across the country to Hollywood, where he became a member of the early western singing group, the Beverly Hill Billies. Soon he became a West Coast radio star, headlining such programs as *Stuart Hamblen and His Lucky Stars*, *Covered Wagon Jubilee*, and *King Cowboy and His Woolly West Review*.

During the 1930s and 1940s, he appeared in western movies with Gene Autry, Roy Rogers, Wild Bill Elliott, and Don "Red" Barry. In 1945 he joined the *Flame of the Barbary Coast* cast, starring John Wayne.

The Calvary Boys took the TCMHOF stage to perform Southern Gospel Music, a key element of Texas Country Music. L to R: Aubrey King, Ronny Meadow, Chris Roberson, Bill Smith.

Although he married in 1933, Stuart drank, gambled, brawled, and wrote such songs as "I Won't Go Huntin' With Ya, Jake, But I'll Go Chasin' Women." Nevertheless, his lovely and devoted wife, Suzy, prayed fervently for him. Stuart finally experienced a religious conversion at the Canvas Cathedral in Los Angeles during the 1949 crusade, bringing fame to evangelist Billy Graham nationwide.

This spiritual turnaround was instrumental in his growing success. Stuart stopped drinking and ran for president in 1952 for the Prohibition Party. He began writing gospel songs and starred in a Sunday morning radio show, *Cowboy Church of the Air*. When Stuart encountered John Wayne on the street, the movie star asked, "What's this I hear about you, Stuart?"

"Well, Duke," answered the transformed Hamblen, "I guess it's no secret what God can do."

"Sounds like a song," commented Wayne.

Groundbreaking ceremony for the new home of the Texas Country Music Hall of Fame, located just west of the original building.

John Wayne's casual remark was a creative inspiration for Hamblen, who composed a gospel classic, "It Is No Secret." Stuart wrote more than 225 other songs, including such hits as "Remember Me," "I'm the One Who Loves You," "Open Up Your Heart and Let the Sunshine In," and "Teach Me, Lord, To Wait." Such artists recorded his songs as Elvis Presley, Johnny Cash, Pat Boone, Eddie Arnold, Hank Snow, and Ernest Tubb. His biggest hit was "This Ole House." Recorded by Rosemary Clooney, "This Ole House" was number one simultaneously in seven countries and was voted the 1954 Song of the Year.

In 1970 Stuart was inducted as a charter member of the Nashville Songwriters Hall of Fame. The following year the Academy of Country and Western Music honored him with its Pioneer Award for being the "first singing country and western cowboy in the history of broadcasting." In 1976 he was awarded a star on the Hollywood Boulevard Walk of Fame, and in 1988 he received a Golden Boot Award for his work in motion pictures.

Stuart and Suzy made their family home at a horse ranch just outside Los Angeles. When he died at the age of eighty on March 8, 1989, he was mourned by his wife, two daughters, ten grandchildren, nineteen great-grandchildren — and countless fans.

A major event of 2002 was the long-anticipated opening of the permanent home of the Texas Country Music Hall of Fame and Museum. Carthage city manager, Charles Thomas, supervised financing and construction contracts. Charles had contacted Neal Hawthorn about the property adjacent to the west of the Tex Ritter Museum/Chamber of Commerce building. Hawthorn promised that Thomas would be first in line when the family was ready to sell the property. After a time, the offer was made, and the City of Carthage purchased the future site of the Texas Country Music Hall of Fame.

Costs of the project would be financed by Certificates of Obligation, which would be sold in the name of the City of Carthage. As a small city (less than 7,500 population), Carthage was permitted to insure its certificates, which would produce a higher rate of return. Accordingly, two corporations were organized: the Carthage Economic Development Corporation [CEDC] and the Carthage Improvement Corporation [CIC]. Charles Thomas was listed as head of both corporations to facilitate the certificate movement.

Construction contracts were awarded to Longview firms: Frith and Associates, architects and planners; and Transit Company, construction manager. An eleven-month construction schedule was announced, but the beginning activity was delayed until the opening of school in 2001.

The City of Carthage was committed to a street project that led to a nearby elementary school. But once Division Street was completed, Firth Associates proceeded immediately. There were no serious weather delays, building materials arrived in a timely fashion, and the superb 13,000-square-foot facility was ready for the induction crowds of 2002.

The 2002 inductees were Tanya Tucker, Gene Watson, and Nat Stuckey. Known as "The Texas Tornado," Tanya Tucker was still a teenager when Elvis Presley caught her show in Denver. Impressed with the pretty, high-energy performer, the King of Rock 'n' Roll blurted: "She's going to be the next Elvis Presley."

"I'd stack any awards in the world up against that one comment," stated Tanya in her 1997 autobiography, *Nickel Dreams*.

* * * *

Tanya Denise Tucker truly was blessed with precocious vocal talents as a child. The youngest of four children, she was born on October 10,

The last gathering at the original Tex Ritter Museum and the Texas Country Music Hall of Fame, before the move next door to the new TCMHOF building.

A major event of 2002 was the long-anticipated opening of the permanent home of the Texas Country Music Hall of Fame and Museum. The impressive new facility was an immediate hit with visitors.

1958, in Seminole, Texas. Tanya's parents, Beau and Juanita Tucker were dogged by poverty. Beau moved the family around as he searched for construction work.

Settling in Willcox, Ariz., for several years, Beau strongly encouraged the musical gifts of his daughters, LaCosta and Tanya. The girls were taken to the performances of touring country artists, and Beau frequently arranged for little Tanya to come onstage and sing. As a result, Tanya, LaCosta, and three Wilcox boys formed a group, the Country Westerners.

The family moved to Phoenix when Tanya was eight, and she became a regular on *The Lew King Ranger Show* on local television. Soon the family moved to Utah, where Tanya landed a non-speaking part in *Jeremiah Johnson*, filmed in 1971 and starring Robert Redford. After another move to Las Vegas, Beau scraped together enough money for a demo tape. A few years earlier, Beau had unsuccessfully peddled a crude demo around Nashville, but this time, Tanya's tape caught the right people's attention.

Thirteen-year-old Tanya Tucker signed a contract with Columbia. She turned down "The Happiest Girl in the USA" in favor of "Delta Dawn," recorded in her first Columbia session. In 1972 "Delta Dawn" reached the top ten, and that same year Tanya made her debut on the *Grand Ole Opry*. She was named the New Female Vocalist of the Year by the Academy of Country Music, and in 1973 she had two number one hits, "What's Your Mama's Name" and "Blood Red and Goin' Down."

In 1974 Beau negotiated a $1.5 million contract with a new label, MCA. The contract was signed on Tanya's sixteenth birthday at a gala party arranged by MCA at a Little Rock amusement park. In 1975 "Lizzie and the Rainman" and "San Antonio Stroll" soared to number one, while "Don't Believe My Heart Can Stand Another You" reached the top five.

There was another number one hit in 1976, "Here's Some Love," along with the top three "You've Got Me to Hold On To." In 1978 the 1975 album, *Tanya Tucker's Greatest Hits*, was certified gold, and her 1978 album, *TNT*, was certified gold within a year.

During this period, Tanya appeared in the motion picture *Hard Country*, with Kim Basinger

Tommie Ritter Smith with Tanya Tucker in 2002.

Than Your Love" reached number one, and in 1988, both "If It Don't Come Easy" and "Strong Enough to Bend" also were number one hits. The 1991 album *What Does I Do With Me* went platinum the following year, while the albums *Can't Run From Yourself* (1992) and *Greatest Hits 1990-1992* (1993) quickly were certified gold.

In 1991 the Country Music Association voted Tanya Female Vocalist of the Year, an honor her legions of fans thought was long overdue. On the night of the CMA Awards, she was in

Tanya Tucker was inducted into the TCMHOF in 2002. The "Texas Tornado" delivered an electrifying performance worthy of her nickname.

and Jan-Michael Vincent, and in the television movies *Amateur Night*, with Dennis Quaid, and *The Rebels*, starring Don Johnson.

By this time, Tanya was a regular on the party scene. She found Los Angeles especially inviting. "There was a party in LA every night, and I figured out I ought to hit every one of them," she said in her autobiography. "I was invited to a lot, and those I wasn't invited to, I'd crash."

A tumultuous romance with Glen Campbell, who was at the height of stardom, gained considerable notoriety. Other romances also were publicized, and her bouts with alcohol and cocaine led to a 1988 stay at the Betty Ford Center for rehabilitation.

Tanya signed with Capitol Records in 1986, quickly hitting number one with "Just Another Love." The following year "I Won't Take Less

the hospital giving birth to her son, Beau; her daughter, Presley, was two years old.

In 1992 she was awarded ACM's Video of the Year for "Two Sparrows in a Hurricane." And in 1991, Tanya, an avid horsewoman, won the Celebrity Cutting Championship in Fort Worth.

Tanya Tucker remains a spectacular performer with a deep love of country music. "As long as anybody wants to listen, I'll be up there singing."

The day before Tanya drove to Carthage for her TCMHOF induction, she and her band broke up over various conflicts. Her partner, Nashville musician Jerry Laseter, scrambled to put together a band as Tanya headed to Carthage. The impromptu band rehearsed on the afternoon of the induction while Tanya stayed on her bus. The drama was in the air as the induction crowd became aware of the situation, and Ralph Emery insisted on seeing Tanya before her induction.

But Tanya exploded onto the stage, beautiful and vivacious and confident. And when her band went out of sync, Tanya took over with the full power of her stardom. The Texas Tornado completely won the crowd and gave one of the most memorable performances in the history of the TCMHOF.

Also, in 2002, Tanya was rated number twentyon CMT's 40 Greatest Women of Country Music, and in 2017 she was named by *Rolling Stone* as one of the 100 Greatest Country Artists of all Time. Additionally, in 2020 Tanya won her first two Grammy Awards for "Bring My Flowers Now" and "While I'm Livin'."

* * * *

When Ann Stuckey took charge of her husband's fan club, she happily distributed badges that declared that the wearer was "Stuck on Stuckey." Indeed, fans were "Stuck on Stuckey" because of Nat's enormous versatility. During a career that spanned more than three decades, Nat Stuckey was a singer, songwriter, deejay, record producer, music publisher, owner of a

Ralph Emery presenting Tanya Tucker with her Hall of Fame plaque. At 13 she was named New Female Vocalist of the Year by the Academy of Country Music, and in 1991 Nashville's Country Music Association voted her Female Vocalist of the Year.

booking agency, and the voice of hundreds of commercials.

This versatile Texan was born in Cass County, Texas, on December 17, 1933. Nathan Wright Stuckey II was raised in Atlanta, Texas, where he learned to play the guitar and developed a deep interest in music. After high school, he attended Arlington State College, where he studied speech and radio-television.

Returning to Atlanta, he became a radio announcer at KALT. After two years, Nat entered the army, working with Armed Services Radio and TV in Korea and New York City. Following his discharge, Nat came back to Atlanta and KALT.

Then he moved to KWKH in Shreveport, home of the *Louisiana Hayride.* Nat worked as a deejay at KWKH for the next eight years, at the same time expanding into other areas of music. In 1957 and 1958, he performed with an eight-piece jazz band. Then Nat formed a country group, the Corn Huskers, and a year later, he became leader of the *Louisiana Hayride.* Nat Stuckey was the last major artist developed by the Hayride.

Nat began recording in 1964, and he was writing songs by this time. In 1966 "Sweet Thang" made the top five, and Loretta Lynn and Ernest Tubb recorded a hit version of the song. Next, Nat wrote "Waitin' in the Welfare Line" for Buck Owens, and the recording spent seven weeks at number one. Finally, in 1967 Jim Ed Brown took Nat's "Pop-a-Top" to the top three.

Nat recorded several songs which hit the charts, and in 1967 he formed a backing band called the Sweet Thangs. In 1969 he reached the top ten with "Sweet Thang and Cisco." Twice he recorded hit duets with Connie Smith, "Young Love" and "If God Is Dead (Who's That Living In My Soul)," and the duo also recorded two albums.

Nat enjoyed a banner year in 1973. "Got Leaving on Her Mind" reached the top fifteen, "Take Time to Love Her" made the top ten, and "I Used It All on You" hit the top three. For a time, Nat's opening act was a fast-rising teenage singer named Tanya Tucker.

During the 1970s, Nat began announcing and singing commercials, eventually recording hundreds of regional and national media ads. He wrote two Coca-Cola jingles, recorded twenty-two McDonald's spots, and became the singing voice of Budweiser commercials.

After Nat and Ann moved to Nashville, they established a booking agency, Music Row Talent, Inc. Nat also bought and sold land in Tennessee and Texas through his Texas Promised Land Development Company.

Despite the demands of his businesses, touring schedule, recording sessions, and songwriting, Nat found time to pursue a variety of personal interests. He rode motorcycles and was a bass fisherman of sufficient skill to be invited to Bass Master tournaments. A dog lover, Nat sometimes was allowed to assist in veterinary surgery (the veterinarian was a business partner). His carpentry skills inspired him to start a woodworking and furniture-making enterprise at his home on Center Hill Lake.

But his last venture was cut short by the discovery of lung cancer. Then, within two months of diagnosis, the fifty-four-year-old entertainer died on August 24, 1988. His ashes were scattered over Center Hill Lake.

Ann Stuckey continued to operate Music Row Talent, Inc., and she placed memorabilia from Nat's life and career in Nashville, at the Louisiana State Exhibit Building in Shreveport, and art museums in Many and Zwolle, La., as well as at the TCMHOF.

* * * *

During his long career in country music, Gene Watson became known as "The Singer's Singer."

"The world stops spinning when he sings," declared Robert K. Oermann, dean of country music critics. "In his voice is all the ache of existence."

The expressive tenor voice of Gene Watson has generated admiration from such stars as George Strait, Marty Robbins, George Jones, and Randy Travis. As a result, he is widely regarded as a singer's singer.

Gary Gene Watson was born on October 11, 1943, in Palestine, Texas. His father was a saw-mill worker and farm laborer. For the first several years of Gene's life, he rambled around with his parents and six brothers and sisters in an old school bus as his father sought work. Often the entire family toiled together harvesting crops.

Finally, the Watsons settled in Paris in northeast Texas. Gene's father was an instrumentalist who liked to play the blues, and the boy quickly developed a feel for music. The family attended Pentecostal church services, and like many budding country artists, young Gene began singing gospel music.

Feeling the need to help support his family, Gene dropped out of school in the ninth grade and found employment as an auto repairman, where he developed a passion for cars. Indeed, Gene still tinkers happily at The Toy Shop, an auto shop he set up for his personal use.

The young husband and father intended to utilize his other passion, music, to supplement his income. So, calling on his musical talents of brothers and cousins, he organized a band, Gene Watson and the Other Four. Gene and his group played clubs around Houston, soon becoming the resident band at the popular Dynasty Club.

Beginning in 1965, Gene and his band recorded for various independent labels. Nearly a decade passed, however, before Gene finally scored a hit. In 1974 the provocative "Love in the Afternoon" was picked up by Capitol Records, and the song reached the top three in 1975. Capitol signed Gene, and with the backing of a major label, he recorded a succession of hits, regularly cracking the top twenty during the next five years. A number of singles charted even higher.

"Where Love Begins" made the top five in 1976, and the next year "Paper Rosie" hit the top three. "I Don't Need a Thing at All" reached

the top ten at the end of 1977, and a year later, "One-Sided Conversation" also made the top ten. In 1979 "Pick the Wildwood Flower" hit the top five, while "Should I Go Home (Or Should I Go Crazy)" reached the top three.

But Gene's favorite hit of 1979 was "Farewell Party." A moving tale of suicide, "Farewell Party" became Gene's signature song, and he named his band after the top three hit.

The next year featured "Nothing Sure Looked Good on You," which reached the top five, and there were three top twenty hits. But after five successful years with Capitol, Gene moved to MCA Records.

His first MCA release, "Between This Time and The Next Time," made the top twenty in 1981. And before the year ended, MCA released Gene's biggest hit, "Fourteen Carat Mind," which reached number one.

During the next three years, Gene enjoyed five top ten hits, a top five, and a top three. He moved to Epic Records in 1985 and immediately reached the top five with "Memories to Burn."

But there was not as much success during the next few years, and by 1988 Gene was considering retirement from the music industry. Then Gene's career was revived by a new manager, Lib Hatcher, who also managed Randy Travis. Lib arranged a contract with Warner Brothers Records. Gene immediately recorded a top five hit, "Don't Waste It on the Blues." Gene also began touring with Randy Travis, who was enjoying the peak of his popularity.

Today, Gene continues to tour with his Farewell Party Band and remains a consummate artist. "I put every song I sing in a different perspective," he says. "I feel each one."

Chapter Five

The Stellar Inductees of 2003-2007

By 2003 the Texas Country Music Hall of Fame had been open for more than half a decade. The handsome new TCMHOF building had received guests for a year and many of the fans arrived by tour bus. Soon the total number of visitors reached 10,000, then 20,000, then 30,000.

Each August since 1998, a parade of country music luminaries spent induction weekend in Carthage. Legendary stars performed and received Hall of Fame plaques, while other famous singers appeared on stage as guest artists. Still, other notables came to pay homage to their country music friends. Everyone who toured the museum was deeply impressed by the collection of artifacts on display and Carthage was on the country music map.

In April 2003, Willie Nelson came through town, and he stopped at the museum. It happened to be April 29, Willie's seventieth birthday, and Tommie Ritter Smith hustled to put together a birthday party for Willie. When Willie learned that Kris Kristofferson was to be approached about induction, he offered to persuade his sometimes reclusive friend to accept, pointing out that the two pals would perform together at the TCMHOF. Indeed, with Lefty Frizzell and Johnny Bush, Kristofferson would lead a stellar trio into the Hall of Fame in 2003.

* * * *

Movie star, groundbreaking songwriter. and Grammy-winning recording artist. Few Texans of any generation have exhibited the multiple talents of Kris Kristofferson.

The son of a US Air Force major general,

Kris was born in Brownsville, Texas, on June 22, 1936. In school, he was an excellent student and athlete. Kris boxed and played football at California's Pomona College, where he majored in creative writing and published award-winning short stories in the prestigious *Atlantic Monthly*. After graduation in 1958, he won a Rhodes Scholarship to Oxford University in England, earning a Master's Degree in English.

Kris attended ranger school, jump school, and flight school to obtain an army commission. He served in Germany as a helicopter pilot, was appointed to the English faculty at West Point, and left the army in 1965 as a captain.

While studying at Oxford, Kris had written rock 'n' roll songs for an English producer. He continued to write after leaving the army, and in 1969 Roger Miller recorded a number of his songs, including "Me and Bobby McGee."

When Janis Joplin covered this song, it sold a million copies. In 1970 Ray Price scored a number one hit and won a Grammy with "For the Good Times," and Johnny Cash turned "Sunday Mornin' Comin' Down" into a number one smash. The next year Sammi Smith brought "Help Me Make It Through the Night" to the top of the charts. The Country Music Association voted it Single of the Year, and Kris won his first Grammy Award for Best Country Song. In 1973 Ronnie Milsap recorded a number one hit with "Please Don't Tell Me How the Story Ends."

With his literary training and the artistry of a poet, Kris wrote songs that reflected the alienation and sexual liberation of the times while

Traveling to an engagement in Shreveport, Willie Nelson stopped in Carthage for a visit to the Texas Country Music Hall of Fame. The date was April 29, 2003 – Willie's 70th birthday. Tommie Ritter Smith quickly put together an impromptu birthday party. Members of the Chamber of Commerce and TCMHOF Board attended, and so did Willie's friend, Ray Price, standing third from left in his shirt sleeves. Willie stands at center, holding the hand of Tommie Ritter Smith.

celebrating honesty and freedom. His spectacular success led to a rapid liberalization of the generally conservative Nashville style of songwriting.

A popular live performer, in 1973, Kris enjoyed a number one hit as a solo artist with "Why Me." That same year his albums, *The Silver Tongued Devil and I* and *Jesus was a Capricorn*, were certified gold. In 1974 his 1971 album, *Me and Bobby McGee*, went gold. In 1978 his compilation album, *Songs of Kristofferson*, also went gold.

Kris married pop singer Rita Coolidge in 1973, and the couple recorded several albums. Their debut album, *Full Moon*, was certified gold in 1975. In 1973 and 1975, they earned Grammys for Best Country Vocal Performance by a Duo or Group: "From the Bottle to the Bottom" and, two years later, "Lover Please."

Kris sang backup to Willie Nelson during the 1979 recording sessions, which produced the album *Willie Nelson Sings Kristofferson*. In 1984 Kris and Willie recorded the album *Music From 'Songwriter.'* The following year Kris, Willie, Waylon Jennings, and Johnny Cash formed a superstar quartet to record *Highwayman*, an album that went gold in 1986. In later years Kris and his pals teamed up for *Highwayman 2* and *Highwayman 3*.

Kris was a natural for the movies with his rugged good looks, lean physique, and gravel voice. His film debut came in 1971 in Dennis Hopper's *The Last Movie*, and he went on to star in more than twenty motion pictures. He played a famous outlaw in *Pat Garrett and Billy the Kid* (1973). When he co-starred with Barbra Streisand in a remake of *A Star Is Born* (1976), Kris provided soundtrack music. The soundtrack album went gold that year and platinum the next, eventually selling more than four million copies. In addition, Kris frequently contributed to other motion picture soundtracks, including films in which he did not appear onscreen.

His film work included starring roles in such

Willie Nelson and Kris Kristofferson spent induction day of 2003 together. The two friends visited with fans, signed autographs, performed onstage, and Willie presented Kris his Hall of Fame plaque.

notable movies as *Alice Doesn't Live Here Anymore* (1974), *Vigilante Force* (1975), *Semi-Tough* (1977), *Convoy* (1978), *Heaven's Gate* (1980), *Rollover* (1981), *Songwriter* (1984), and *Millennium* (1989). In 1999 he played a crime boss opposite Mel Gibson in *Payback*. Onscreen, Kris has effectively portrayed westerners, athletes, good guys, bad guys, romantic leads, and various other characters.

Married three times, Kris is the father of eight children. He makes his home in Southern California and continues to practice his exceptional gifts as a musician and actor. In Carthage, Kris received a wild reception from an adoring crowd.

* * * *

David Frizzell represented his older brother, Lefty, on the TCMHOF stage. David toured as a teenager during the 1950s with Lefty Frizzell. The brothers worked together into the 1960s before Da-

vid achieved stardom during the 1980s, often alongside Shelly West. By that time, Lefty Frizzell was a country music icon.

"When I sing," explained Lefty Frizzell not long before his premature death, "to me, every word had a feeling about it. I had to linger, had to hold it. I didn't want to let go of it. I want to hold one word through a whole line of melody, to linger with it all the way down. I didn't want to let go of that no more than I wanted to let go of the woman I loved."

Frizzell did not often try to analyze his distinctive and influential singing style, but many other artists and music critics have. "I feel that he was the most unique thing that has ever happened to country music," flatly stated Merle Haggard. Similar praise also came from such superstars as Willie Nelson, George Jones, Randy Travis, and George Strait.

"Lefty Frizzell was the most definitive honky tonk singer, the vocalist that set the style for generations of vocalists that followed him," according to Stephen Thomas Erlewine in *All Music Guide to Country*. "Frizzell smoothed out the

Tommie Ritter Smith with two of the 2003 inductees, Kris Kristofferson and Johnny Bush. (Lefty Frizzell was the third inductee, with a posthumous award.)

Willie Nelson had the pleasure of presenting a Hall of Fame plaque to Johnny Bush.

growing family to El Dorado, Ark., when his oldest boy, "Sonny," was fourteen. Soon goaded into a schoolyard fight, the new kid beat his opponent with a devastating left hand, and Sonny Frizzell acquired the nickname "Lefty."

By this time, the teenager, attracted to country music by the Jimmie Rodgers records of his parents, was singing professionally. Lefty landed a radio job over KELD in El Dorado, and when the family moved back to Texas, he took a similar gig on KPTL in Paris. Lefty regularly played dances and nightclubs, and he began appearing on KGFL in Roswell, N. M.

But his promising musical career was interrupted by a run-in with this law, and Lefty went to work with his father in the oil fields. Soon he gravitated back to music, by 1950 settling in at the Ace of Clubs in San Angelo, where he developed an enthusiastic fan base.

In 1950 Lefty signed with Columbia Records. His first session produced "If You've Got the Money, I've Got the Time" and "I Love You a Thousand Ways." Both sides of this first record reached number one, and Lefty's career soared meteorically.

In 1951 he organized a backup group, the Western Cherokees. As a result, Lefty had four recordings in the top ten for a time, a feat that has never been surpassed. "I Want to Be with You Always," on his third record, spent eleven weeks at number one, and his next release, "Always Late (With Your Kisses)," was at number one for twelve weeks.

rough edges of honky tonk by singing longer, flowing phrases — essentially, he made honky tonk more acceptable for the mainstream without losing its gritty bar-room roots . . . Frizzell's singing became the foundation of how hard country should be sung."

"What set Lefty apart from other singers was what he did with his voice," explained author Paul Kingsbury in *The Grand Ole Opry History of Country Music*. "He bent notes as if his vocal cords were guitar strings, stretched single syllables into several, pushed against the upper and lower edges of his warm baritone for effects both rough and tender. Like a blues singer, he took his good sweet time singing each and every line."

William Orville R.C. Frizzell was born on March 31, 1928, in Corsicana, Texas, the first of eight children. Naaman Orville, R.C. Frizzell's father was an oil field worker who moved his

David Frizzell (center) performed in honor of his older brother, Lefty Frizzell. Ralph Emery (right) presented Lefty's plaque to David.

drinking problem, he developed high blood pressure, but he refused to take blood pressure medicine, and on July 19, 1975, he died of a stroke in Nashville at the age of forty-seven.

Lefty was inducted into the Country Music Hall of Fame in 1982. And as emphasized by Stephen Thomas Erlewine, "The greatest testament to his music remains the fact that his voice can be heard in every hard country singer that has followed."

* * * *

Lefty continued to record top ten hits during 1951 and 1952 when he was invited to join the *Grand Ole Opry*. But he chafed at being restricted to the Opry on weekends, which offered the most lucrative road appearance possibilities. So Lefty quit the Opry, and he fired his manager and his band.

Moving to Los Angeles, he became a regular on Tex Ritter's television show, *Town Hall Party*. Then, Lefty's younger brother, David, hitchhiked to California. Lefty hired him and arranged a recording contract with Columbia, and eventually, David Frizzell became a star in his own right.

Lefty composed 300 songs, but few of his recordings were hits after 1952. Although still immensely popular on the road, he spent money as rapidly as he earned it. Lefty and his wife, Alic, had four children.

Not long after *Town Hall Party* ended in 1960, Lefty moved his family to Nashville. Even though his career seemed to lack direction, "Saginaw, Michigan" spent four weeks at number one in 1964.

It was Lefty's last big hit. In addition to a

Another masterful country singer, Johnny Bush — "The Country Caruso" — also was inducted into the TCMHOF in 2003.

"If I wasn't getting paid for this, I'd be doing it anyway," stated singer-songwriter-instrumentalist Johnny Bush. "It's what I do."

He began doing it as a boy. Born John Bush Shin III in Houston on February 17, 1935, he grew up listening to his father, and other relatives and friends make music in the Shin home. They sang and played guitars and fiddles, and Johnny avidly listened to country music over the radio. "I would go to the movies on Saturdays and hear Roy Rogers sing," reminisced Johnny, "and I thought, that's me, boy."

Johnny's father taught him guitar chords when he was ten; within two years, he was singing and playing in public. In 1952, when Johnny was seventeen, he landed a gig performing with the Texas Star Playboys every weekend at the Texas Star Inn in San Antonio and on a local country television show.

One night the drummer failed to show up, and Johnny was pressed into service. He quickly took to the drum set. "I found out there was a shortage of drummers," explained Johnny. "Everybody sang and played guitar. But a drummer could work."

Soon the band hired a young guitarist named Willie Nelson, and Johnny and Willie became lifelong friends. Johnny played and sang with Texas legends Bob Wills and Lefty Frizzell, working barrooms, dancehalls, and honky tonks. When Willie Nelson formed his first band, The Offenders, Johnny came aboard as a drummer.

Johnny gravitated to Nashville and joined Ray Price's band, the Cherokee Cowboys. Working closely with Price for three years, he was strongly influenced by Ray's singing style. Indeed, when Johnny tried to land a recording contract, one label after another felt that he sounded too much like Price.

But Willie Nelson financed Johnny's first album, *Sound of a Heartache*. In 1967 Johnny enjoyed his first hit, "You Oughta Hear Me Cry." There were three hits the following year, including "Undo the Right," which broke the top ten. After reaching the top twenty in 1972 with "I'll Be There," Johnny signed a recording contract with RCA.

The powerhouse label intended to showcase the promising vocalist with the nickname "The Country Caruso." Asked to provide songs for his first album with RCA, Johnny was returning to Texas from Nashville on his tour bus. Awakening in Texarkana, the lines of "Whiskey River" began to run through his mind. His recording broke the top ten in 1972. Willie Nelson later adopted "Whiskey River" as his theme song, making more than twenty different recordings.

But in 1972, on the verge of stardom, Johnny was stricken with a mysterious, debilitating condition that produced spasms in his vocal cords. Johnny consulted numerous specialists, even seeing a psychiatrist and a chiropractor, but his voice rapidly worsened. He could speak only in a strangled whisper, and his singing voice made a mockery of the nickname "Country Caruso."

So RCA dropped him from their label.

Finally, after several nightmarish years, a San Antonio speech therapist diagnosed his affliction as spasmodic dysphonia, a rare neurological condition that causes the vocal cords to short circuit. Although told there was no cure, in 1985, Johnny began working with Gary Catona, a University of Texas vocal teacher. Employing various innovative techniques, Catona dramatically improved Johnny's vocal capabilities. (Based on this success, Catona went on to work with a parade of famous clients: Liza Minelli, Tony Bennett, Paula Abdul, Brian Wilson, Andy Williams, Shirley MacLaine, Jack Klugman, Kevin Spacey, and Mohammed Ali.)

Regaining perhaps eighty percent of his previous vocal abilities, Johnny eagerly resumed his performing and recording career and began earning a variety of comeback awards. "I think that God put this on me for a reason, and I think that reason is to help others." Having picked up a career that seemed lost, Johnny bristles when asked about retirement. "Retire from what? Breathing? People only retire from jobs they hate. Performing is not a job. It's what I do."

And the "Country Caruso" continued to sing until the end of his life. Johnny Bush died of pneumonia in a San Antonio hospital in 2020 or at the age of eighty-five.

After just six years, the Texas Country Music Hall of Fame boasted twenty-two, stellar inductees. At the TCMHOF, country music fans could examine a dazzling array of memorabilia and visit the impressive statues of Tex Ritter and Jim Reeves. And in 2004, three more stars were added: Mac Davis, Johnny Lee, and "The Big Bopper" — J.P. Richardson.

* * * *

Like a few of the previous inductees, Mac Davis had starred in motion pictures and television shows as well as in the music world. Growing up in Lubbock, Mac heard mostly country music into his teens.

"When I was growing up in West Texas, we didn't have rock 'n' roll," stated Mac, reflecting on his long and varied career. "I'd always listened to country music. That's my roots. I'd never heard anything but country music — Hank Williams, Eddy Arnold, and Ernest Tubb — until I was thirteen or so.

In addition to widespread recognition as a country artist-songwriter, Mac Davis has also enjoyed success in pop music, Broadway, movies, and television. But through all of his entertainment activities, Mac's country roots consistently are reflected in his soft West Texas twang.

Scott "Mac" Davis was born in Lubbock on January 21, 1942. Musically inclined, "I was probably making up melodies when I was only five or six years old."

Mac sang in the church choir, and he learned to play the blues harp, bongo drums, and guitar. Like countless other teenagers during the 1950s, Elvis Presley strongly influenced Mac.

But he did not focus on his musical abilities. "At this point, my grades had degenerated, and I was just a hoodlum." Restlessly in 1957, Mac left "Texas in My Rearview Mirror" and moved to Atlanta, Georgia.

Mac Davis sat on a stool, picked up his guitar – and utterly charmed the TCMHOF audience. Davis hosted a television variety show during the 1970s, was featured in such movies as *North Dallas Forty* and the *Sting II*, and starred on Broadway in the *Will Rogers Follies*. Elvis Presley, Glen Campbell, Kenny Rogers and other artists recorded Mac Davis songs.

Display at the TCMHOF Museum honoring the 2004 inductees. L to R: Johnny Lee, Mac Davis, and the Big Bopper, J.P. Richardson.

Soon he organized a rock 'n' roll band, sometimes performing tunes to his own compositions. Next, he became a regional manager for Vee-Jay Records, then moved to Los Angeles in 1967 as head of the Liberty publishing label.

Mac's songwriting breakthrough came in 1968 when Elvis Presley recorded "A Little Less Conversation." Elvis wanted more Davis songs, and during the next couple of years, Presley scored hits with "Memories," "In the Ghetto," and "Don't Cry Daddy."

Glen Campbell, Kenny Rogers, and numerous other

artists eagerly recorded Mac Davis songs. Mac's sentimental songs about his little boy, "Watching Scotty Grow" and "Daddy's Little Man," were hits for Bobby Goldsboro.

Mac signed with Columbia Records as an artist in 1970, and two years later, he recorded a number one pop hit with "Baby Don't Get Hooked On Me." He charted repeatedly during the 1970s and 1980s. Two memorable hits of 1980 were "It's Hard to Be Humble" and "Texas in My Rearview Mirror." In 1991 Mac's *Greatest Hits* album went gold.

From 1974-76 Mac hosted a TV variety show, and in 1974 he was named AMC Entertainer of the Year. In 1979 he played a Dallas Cowboy quarterback based on Don Meredith in *North Dallas Forty*, and four years later, Mac again was featured on big screens in *The Sting II* with Jackie Gleason. In addition, he starred on Broadway in *The Will Rogers Follies* and other Hollywood and televison movies. For decades Mac Davis has demonstrated Hall of Fame talent and versatility.

At the TCMHOF, Mac sat on a stool with his guitar, taking requests from the audience and even making up a humorous song. The TCMHOF crowd was captivated by Mac Davis.

* * * *

"Hellooo . . . Baby!"

The deep, rich voice that uttered the opening line to "Chantilly Lace" belonged to Jiles Perry Richardson, Jr., known to fans as The Big Bopper. But The Big Bopper's meteoric rise to fame was cut short by one of the most stunning tragedies ever to strike the music world.

Born in Sabine Pass, Texas, on October 24, 1930, the husky youngster moved with his family and played football at Beaumont High School. After high school graduation in 1949, he served a stint in the army and earned a diploma from a technical school in radio and TV broadcasting.

In 1955 Richardson became a deejay in KTRM in Beaumont, a station where he had worked be-

J.P. Richardson, son of the Big Bopper, represented his father at the 2004 induction.

fore joining the army. He was a wild man on the air, and *The Big Bopper Show* attracted a strong fan base while providing Richardson with a popular stage name. In May 1957, he set a world record for continuous broadcasting, with his *Discathon* remaining on the air for six straight days while he spun 1,821 records.

But success as a deejay did not satisfy the musical ambitions of The Big Bopper. Influenced by country and western music, he began writing songs, then shifted toward the new sound of rockabilly. During an abbreviated career as a songwriter, he composed about thirty-eight tunes and recorded more than twenty of them. Among his recordings were "Crazy Blues" and "Beggar to a King," which later was a hit for Hank Snow. In addition, Richardson's "Running Bear" would become a hit for Johnny Preston.

"Chantilly Lace" was released on Mercury Records in the summer of 1958 and soared to number six on the pop charts. Suddenly The Big Bopper — "Hello . . . Baby!" — was known nationwide, and he intended to capitalize on the opportunity. So The Big Bopper took a leave of absence from KTRM to go on tour. His stage performances were flamboyant, featuring zoot suits and a prop phone for "Chantilly Lace."

Early in 1959, he joined *The Winter Tour* with Buddy Holly as the headliner for a three-week series of appearances in the upper midwest. But the bus developed engine trouble, the heater stopped working, and The Big Bopper fell ill under the frigid temperatures.

On the night of February 2, Buddy Holly, Richie Valens, and The Big Bopper played the Surf Ballroom in Clear Lake, Iowa. Holly chartered a three-passenger plane to avoid a long bus ride to North Dakota. The Big Bopper, hoping to have time to see a doctor, persuaded Holly's sideman, Waylon Jennings, to give up his seat on the plane.

An hour after midnight, the plane took off but immediately crashed and cartwheeled. The Big Bopper, Buddy Holly, Richie Valens, and the pilot died instantly. Only twenty-eight, The Big Bopper was flown back to Beaumont for funeral services.

At his death, "The Big Bopper's Wedding" was climbing the charts. Richardson had married Adrian Joy Fryon in 1952. They had a daughter, Deborah, and Adrian was pregnant when the Big Bopper was killed. Jay P. Richardson never knew his father, but for the past several years, he has recreated The Big Bopper performance on television and live performances. His recreation of The Big Bopper certainly was a hit with TCM-HOF fans.

* * * *

"I love a good country song," declared singer Johnny Lee, a Texas farm boy during the 1950s, "but I can get sentimental about some of the old fifties stuff."

Destined to vault to stardom during the

Johnny Lee was besieged by autograph seekers.

a 1979 TV movie. He followed up the next year with a small role in John Travolta's Hollywood hit, *Urban Cowboy*. While the soundtrack album soared to triple platinum, Johnny's single release, "Lookin' for Love," climbed to number one and was certified platinum. An album of the same title was certified gold and produced another number one single, "One in a Million."

In 1981 Johnny released his second album, *Bet Your Heart on Me*, and the title song hit number one. He reached the top three with "Pickin' Up Strangers" and "Prisoner of Hope." Johnny received the 1981 Best New Male Vocalist Award

2004 guest performer, Little Jimmy Dickens. Standing an inch under five feet, Dickens became a popular singing and comedic performer at the *Grand Ole Opry*.

1980s, Johnny Lee was born John Lee Ham in Texas City on July 3, 1946. While growing up on a dairy farm near Alta Loma, he organized "Johnny Lee and the Roadrunners." However, Johnny Lee's musical career took a back seat for four years during the 1960s after he joined the navy, serving aboard a guided missile cruiser in Vietnamese waters.

Following his discharge, Johnny joined Mickey Gilley's band as a singer and trumpet player. With the opening of Gilley's Club in Pasadena in 1971, Johnny headlined the band when Mickey was on tour. Launching a recording career in the mid-1970s, he occasionally made the country charts with such singles as "Red Sails in the Sunset," "Ramblin' Rose," and "Country Party."

Tall and handsome, Johnny landed a role in

Whispering Bill Anderson, 2004 guest performer.

and left Gilley's to form the Western Union Band. He installed his new group in his Pasadena club, Johnny Lee's. He also established the Johnny Lee Pro-Am Golf Tournament to aid the mentally handicapped through the Home of Guiding Hands.

Johnny enjoyed a fine recording year in 1983, hitting the top three with "Hey Bartender" and the top ten with "Sounds Like Love." In addition, there were two number one in 1984, "You Could've Heard a Heart Break" and "The Yellow Rose," a duet with Lane Brody.

At the height of his success in 1982, Johnny Lee married Charlene Tilton, the beautiful blonde actress who was one of the stars of the TV series *Dallas*. For the next couple of years, Johnny and Charlene were regularly targeted by the tabloids, and they divorced in 1984.

Two years later, Johnny wed Debbie Lee, but she died after a lengthy illness. Nevertheless, by Charlene, Johnny's daughter Cherish and his son, Johnny Jr., gave him deep pride: "I can't even express how much I truly love them."

Sadly, Johnny Lee, Jr. died in 2014 of a drug overdose, vaulting his father into the battle against illegal drugs.

"Like many people, I am a work in progress," said Lee. "I work daily to be a better person in all areas of my life, and I think my music reflects that growth."

At his TCMHOF induction in 2004, Johnny Lee scored an unforgettable moment by telephoning President George W. Bush on stage and receiving congratulations from the President.

Although it was impossible to sustain the success he enjoyed during the 1980s, in 1996, Johnny was named Veteran Music Singer of the Year for his gospel recording, "He Could Have Walked On By." And in 2008, Johnny Lee began performing in Branson, Mo.

In 2005, for the first time in six years, four artists were inducted into the TCMHOF: Jimmy Dean, Roger Miller, Johnny Gimble, and Glenn Sutton.

* * * *

When Jimmy Dean was welcomed to the Texas Country Music Hall of Fame stage, the internationally famous star took command of the audience in a way that suggested the fulfillment of his boyhood dreams.

"I dreamt of havin' a beautiful home, a nice car, and nice clothes," he reminisced to a *TV Guide* reporter, referring to his poverty-stricken boyhood in West Texas. "I wanted to be somebody."

To countless television and country music fans, the West Texas farm boy became the "Dean

Jimmy Dean commanded the stage and the audience during the 2005 ceremony. Dean became the first country artist to play the Las Vegas Strip, and he graced such high profile stages as the Hollywood Bowl, the London Palladium, and Carnegie Hall. His movie roles included the villain opposite Sean Connery in *Diamonds are Forever*.

of Country Music" in the wake of his 1961 mega-hit, "Big Bad John." Dean wrote the ballad while flying from New York to Nashville. His recording sold more than eight million copies, leading to television stardom and other hits.

Born near Plainview, Texas, on August 10, 1928, Jimmy worked on neighboring farms to add a little income to the family purse. His mother taught him to play the piano when he was ten, and the boy soon began learning the accordion, guitar, and harmonica.

As a teenager, Jimmy joined the merchant marines, and following a two-year hitch, he enlisted in the air force. He enjoyed entertaining his buddies, and while stationed at Bolling Air Force Base near Washington, D.C., he joined a band, the Tennessee Haymakers. He became a popular attraction at service and civilian clubs, and after his discharge, he stayed in the D.C. area, forming another band, the Texas Wildcats.

In 1952 Jimmy toured US military bases in the Caribbean, made his first recordings, and began appearing on local TV around Washington. In 1957 CBS brought Jimmy to New York City to star in a live country music show early each morning. That same year he signed a recording contract with Columbia Records.

After the blockbuster success of "Big Bad John," Jimmy recorded other narrative ballads, of which the most popular was "PT 109," about President Kennedy's naval exploits in World War II. By 1966, when he switched labels from Columbia to RCA, Jimmy had capitalized on his recording success to launch a career in network television.

From 1963 to 1966, *The Jimmy Dean Show* aired on Thursday evenings over ABC-TV. Presenting country music with class and easy charm, Jimmy introduced to a national audience such country stars as George Jones, Patsy Cline, Roger Miller, Roy Clark, and Buck Owens, along with Jim Henson and his Muppets. Jimmy also was a popular guest host for Johnny Carson, Merv Griffin, Mike Douglas, Dinah Shore, and Joey Bishop.

Turning to acting, Jimmy played a recurring role, Josh Clements, on the hit TV series *Daniel Boone*, from 1967 to 1970. In 1971, he played opposite Sean Connery in a James Bond movie, *Diamonds Are Forever*.

Jimmy became the first country artist to play the Las Vegas strip. He also has graced such high-profile stages as the Hollywood Bowl, the London Palladium, and Carnegie Hall.

At the height of his popularity, in 1968, he founded the Jimmy Dean Meat Company in Plainview, and from his appearances in commer-

Jimmy Dean signing autographs.

In 2005 Carthage Mayor Carson Joines, assisted by Tommie Ritter Smith, Sharon Richardson (president of the Tex Ritter Fan Club), Ida Beck, and Lynn Vincent, presided over the designation of "Tex Ritter Drive" and "Jim Reeves Drive."

gine #9." "Do-Wacha-Do." "Me and Bobby McGee."

This partial list of song hits only suggests the colossal success enjoyed by Roger Miller, a native Texan who was voted into Nashville's Country Music Hall of Fame in 1995.

A gifted, imaginative songwriter who wrote most of his hits as a performer, Roger's songs also were recorded by such stars as Jim Reeves, George Jones, Loretta Lynn, Jimmy Dean, Ernest Tubb, Andy Williams, Jan Howard, Rex Allen, Faron Young, Johnny Paycheck, Willie Nelson, and duo artists David Frizzell and Shelly West.

Roger became a superstar during the 1960s. At the 1964 Grammy Awards, he collected five Grammys: Best New Country & Western Artist, Best Country & Western Album (*Roger Miller*), Best Country & Western Single, Best Country & Western Song ("Dang Me"), and Best Country & Western Performance, Male.

The following year Roger collected an unprecedented six Grammys. "King of the Road" triggered five awards: Best Country & Western Single, Best Contemporary (R&R) Single, Best Country & Western Song, Best Country & Western Performance, Male, and Best Contemporary (R&R) Vocal Performance. In addition, his sixth Grammy of 1965 was presented for Best Country & Western Album (*The Return of Roger Miller*).

Roger was a delightful humorist who made guest television appearances on *The Tonight Show* and *The Jimmy Dean Show*. During the

cials, he became known as "The Sausage King." Jimmy had two sons and a daughter from his first marriage, and in 1991 he wed Donna Meade, a former recording artist, and songwriter. In 2004 Jimmy and Donna collaborated on his autobiography, *Thirty Years of Sausage, Fifty Years of Ham*.

In 2010, at the age of eighty-one, Jimmy Dean died quietly at his estate in Virginia. He was interred on the estate inside a nine-foot-tall, piano-shaped mausoleum. Dean's epitaph is "Here Lies One Hell of a Man," a paraphrased lyric from his mega-hit, "Big Bad John."

* * * *

"King of the Road." "Dang Me." "Chug-a-Lug." "When Two Worlds Collide." "Engine En-

1966-67 season, he starred in a variety hour, *The Roger Miller Show*. In 1974 Roger was the voice of Rooster in the Disney animated movie *Robin Hood*, for which he wrote the music.

During the 1980s, this multifaceted artist turned his talents to Broadway. In eighteen months, he created the musical *Big River*, based on Mark Twain's classic American novel, *The Adventures of Huckleberry Finn*. Opening on Broadway in 1985, *Big River* collected seven Tony Awards and represented the crowning achievement of Roger's career. When *Big River* played Nashville, Roger took the part of Pap, Huckleberry's father.

Roger Dean Miller was born in Fort Worth on January 2, 1936. But during his boyhood, his father died, and the family split up. Roger was sent to the Oklahoma cotton farm of an uncle. Musically gifted, young Roger learned to play the guitar, fiddle, and drums. As a teenager, he hooked up with various bands and played honky tonks in Oklahoma and Texas.

Drafted into the army, he soon was assigned to a hillbilly band by a special forces officer. While in the army, he met Bill Anderson and the brother of performer Jethro Burns. Roger was encouraged to go to Nashville, where his career soared.

Married three times and the father of eight children, Roger contracted throat cancer in 1991. His third wife, Mary, provided staunch companionship until he died, on October 25, 1992, at fifty-six.

An unpredictable genius, Roger Miller was nicknamed "The Wild Thing." And another talented musician and humorist, Roy Clark, said of Roger, "When they made him, they threw away the gyroscope."

At the 2005 TCMHOF induction, Roger Miller was represented by his son Dean, a singer-songwriter from Nashville.

* * * *

Like Tex Ritter, Jim Reeves, and Linda Davis,

Glenn Sutton, who attended school for several years in Carthage, penned major hits for Tammy Wynette, Jerry Lee Lewis, David Houston, and Lynn Anderson.

Glenn Sutton spent several years in Carthage public schools before finding fame and success in country music.

Royce Glenn Sutton was born on September 28, 1937, in Hodge, La., but the family soon moved to East Texas. Glenn began writing his first song as a fourth-grader at Carthage where he attended elementary school and junior high. Glenn started high school in Henderson but graduated after the family moved to Jackson, Miss.

By this time, Glenn had become adept at several instruments, including the guitar, mandolin, drums, piano, trumpet, bass, and steel guitar. Selling insurance by day, after dark, he played clubs in and around Jackson.

Glenn's first recordings were cut in Tyler at Robin Hood Brian's Recording Studio and brought to the attention of Merle Kilgore in Nashville. By 1964 Glenn was sufficiently encouraged to try his luck in Nashville as a songwriter. Almost immediately, he scored a hit when Hank Williams, Jr., covered "Guess What, That's Right, She's Gone."

Also, in 1964 Glenn began a songwriting partnership with Billy Sherrill that produced an impressive string of hits during the 1960s and 1970s. Merle Kilgore signed the team to Al Gallico Music in 1966, and Charlie Walker promptly scored a top forty single, followed by David Houston, who provided Glenn and Billy with their first number one for "Almost Persuaded."

Glenn Sutton thanking Lynn Anderson for singing his hits at the TCMHOF induction.

Dynamic Lynn Anderson was a star of the 2005 induction program. A former wife who remained a close friend of inductee Glenn Sutton, Anderson belted out the songwriter's greatest hits, many of which had been written for her.

The team then won a 1966 Grammy for Best Country & Western Song.

David Houston continued recording Sutton-Sherrill tunes in 1967, hitting number one with "You Mean the World to Me" and "With One Exception." Tammy Wynette recorded a number one in 1967 with "I Don't Wanna Play House" and in 1968 with "Take Me to Your World." Also, in 1968 David Houston enjoyed two number one hits with "Have a Little Faith" and "Already It's Heaven." Tammy Wynette scored two more number one songs in 1969, "Singin' My Song" and "The Ways to Love a Man," as well as a 1971 number one "Bedtime Story" and a 1973 number one, "Kids Say the Darndest Things."

In 1968 Jerry Lee Lewis hit number one with a pair of songs penned solely by Glenn, "What Made Milwaukee Famous (Has Made a Loser Out of Me)" and "She Still Comes Around (To Love What's Left of Me.)"

Also, in 1968, Glenn married his first wife, singer Lynn Anderson, and they would have a daughter, Lisa Lynn. By this time, Glenn had begun producing recording sessions, and in 1970 he took over production duties for his wife. During the next few years, Lynn recorded a number of her husband's songs, hitting number one in 1971 with "You're My Mind" and 1973 with "Keep Me in Mind."

Numerous artists, from George Jones to Charlie Rich, from Merle Haggard to Glenn Campbell, also recorded Sutton Hits. Glenn Sutton received twenty-seven BMI Awards, including Producer of the Year. He also wrote the theme and background music for the Benny Hill television show and music for the movie soundtrack for *Thelma and Louise*.

Along with Tex and Gentleman Jim and lovely Linda, Carthage is proud to claim master songwriter Glenn Sutton. And in Carthage, at his TCMHOF induction, Glenn's hit songs were performed on stage by his beautiful former wife, country star Lynn Anderson.

Fiddler Johnny Gimble performing at his 2005 induction.

* * * *

Legendary fiddler Johnny Gimble played with Bob Wills, the Texas Playboys, and Louisiana Governor Jimmie Davis. An elite sideman in Nashville during the 1960s and the 1970s, he was named CMA Instrumentalist of the Year five times and Fiddler of the Year by the Academy of Country Music eight times. Not content to master the standard four-string fiddle, he also decided to employ a five-string fiddle, naming his instruments "Ole Red" and "Five."

Born in Tyler on May 20, 1926, Johnny and his four brothers were raised in East Texas' Rose City. The five musical brothers — Johnny, Gene, Jerry, Jack, and Bill — played various local gigs. Johnny mastered the fiddle and the mandolin and banjo, and sometimes he sang. While still a student at Tyler High School, Johnny organized the Rose City Swingsters with two of his brothers and a friend. The Swingsters played on KGKB Radio in Tyler, and in 1943 Johnny went to Shreveport to play over KWKH, accompanying Governor Jimmie Davis with his campaign band.

At the end of World War II, Johnny joined the US Army. After his discharge, he returned to Texas and, in 1949, Johnny married Barbara Kemp. The couple has three children: a son, twin daughters, and four grandchildren.

The same year he married, Johnny joined the Texas Playboys, playing and recording with Wills off and on for nearly a decade. When Wills died in 1975, Johnny played at the funeral. Later Johnny was co-leader of a Wills revival band, Playboys II, and in 1982 he portrayed Bob in the Clint Eastwood motion picture, *Honky Tonk Man*.

In 1968 Johnny moved to Nashville and became a top session player, playing on countless recordings. His fiddle and mandolin backed Merle Haggard, Charley Pride, George Jones and Tammy Wynette, Porter Waggoner and Dolly Parton, Conway Twitty and Loretta Lynn, George Strait, and even Paul McCartney and Joan Baez.

Johnny made numerous appearances on TV as a staff fiddler on *Good Ole Nashville Music*, as a member of the *Hee Haw* "Million Dollar Band," and as a performer on *Nashville Now*, *Prime Time Country*, and *Austin City Limits*. A member of Willie Nelson's touring band from 1979-1981, he also appeared with Willie in the 1980 movie *Honeysuckle Rose*.

Johnny produced several albums, beginning with *Fiddlin' Around* in 1974 and including *Still*

Fiddlin' Around in 1988. He moved back to Texas in the 1980s, headquartering in Dripping Springs and leading his band, Texas Swing. Johnny's band featured his son, Dick Gimble, on bass.

In 1995 Johnny was declared a national treasure by the National Endowment for the Arts. He overcame a series of strokes late in 1999 to resume his artistry on the fiddle, and he continued to play as an octogenarian.

"It's still fun," smiled Johnny. "I look forward to the next gig."

One of his proudest gigs was at the TCM-HOF, where the crowd enthusiastically received him. Johnny served an appointed term as State Musician of Texas, and so did his granddaughter Emily Gimble, who often performed with Johnny as a vocalist and keyboardist. Indeed, Johnny's son Dick and his granddaughter Emily performed onstage at the Texas Country Music Hall of Fame induction. In 2015 Johnny Gimble died at his home in Dripping Springs at the age of eighty-eight.

In 2006 the Texas Country Music Hall of Fame inducted two acts — and four artists. The noted songwriter-performer Billy Joe Shaver was a 2006 inductee, and so were the Gatlin Brothers — Larry, Steve, and Rudy.

* * * *

"Billy Joe Shaver may be the best songwriter alive today," pronounced his friend and collaborator, Willie Nelson.

Shaver's songs have been recorded by an impressive array of artists, including Willie Nelson, Waylon Jennings, Elvis Presley, Patty Loveless, the Oak Ridge Boys, Tom T. Hall, and Bob Dylan.

"He's as real a writer as Hemingway," said Kris Kristofferson. "He's timeless."

The timeless songs of Billy Joe Shaver flow from the soul of a country boy who has endured hardship and tragedy. Born in Corsicana, Texas, on September 15, 1941, he was abandoned by his father before his birth. As an infant, Billy Joe was left with his impoverished grandmother when

Genial Billy Joe Shaver proudly posing with his Hall of Fame plaque.

his mother moved to Waco. He spent boyhood summers chopping cotton on farms outside Corsicana.

Billy Joe's grandmother died when he was twelve. He moved to his mother's home near Waco but clashed with her new husband. The unhappy youngster spent a great deal of time away from home at the honky tonk where his mother worked or at a nearby hobo camp. Billy Joe picked up rough habits and was often in trouble for fighting.

He quit school in the eighth grade, but not before impressing an English teacher with his talent for writing verse. He never forgot her encouragement. "As long as you are honest with what you write, you will always have something special to say."

At seventeen, he enlisted in the US Navy. Following his discharge, he returned to Waco and soon met Brenda Tindall. Billy Joe and Brenda married and had a son, Eddy. Billy Joe worked at a sawmill and cowboyed on his father-in-law's ranch. Although an accident at the sawmill cost him two fingers on his right hand, he continued to play guitar.

Shaver played and sang in honky tonks, and several times he traveled to Nashville to try to sell the songs he was writing. Unfortunately, his marriage became strained, and Billy Joe and Brenda divorced, but later remarried. Shaver drank heavily and abused drugs. But his personal travails provided heartfelt material for his songs, which rang true for country music fans.

Noted artists began recording Shaver songs, and in 1973 *Honky Tonk Heroes*, perhaps the best of all Waylon Jennings albums was almost entirely composed of Billy Joe's materials. That same year Kris Kristofferson produced *Old Five and Dimers Like Me*, Shaver's first album. Other albums followed, most notably *I'm Just an Old Lump of Coal, But I'm Gonna Be a Diamond Some Day* in 1980.

Eddy Shaver, a talented guitarist, played in Billy Joe's band. Like his father, he struggled with drug and alcohol problems, and Eddy died at thirty-eight of a heroin overdose in 2000. A year earlier, Brenda Shaver died of cancer.

But Billy Joe continued to write songs, and in 2005 he published his autobiography, *Honky Tonk Hero*. That same year, he married Wanda Lynn Canady, who remained at his side for the rest of his life.

"To me, the song is poetry," reflected Shaver about his art. "It's how I describe the world around me, make sense of it. When I lost my fingers, Jesus made it clear to me that writing songs is my life mission. I've stayed true to that ever since, and I always will. I believe my songs will live long after I'm gone."

Billy Joe Shaver died of a massive stroke in 2020 at the age of eighty-one. And many of his artfully crafted songs do indeed live on.

* * * *

The 2006 TCMHOF crowd eagerly anticipated Larry, Steve, and Rudy Gatlin, and the talented brother trio repeatedly generated heartfelt applause. Indeed, the Gatlins had been capturing the hearts of audiences since they were little boys.

Six-year-old Larry Wayne Gatlin was scheduled to sing at the 1955 *Cavalcade of Talent* held in Abilene, Texas. Larry's sister, LaDonna, had heard him singing with their little brothers, and she persuaded their mother to put all three brothers onstage. As a result, Larry was joined by four-year-old Steve and two-year-old Rudy in the first public performance of the Gatlin brothers. The following year the Gatlin brothers won the *Cavalcade of Talent* — the beginning of a lifetime of triumphs for the musically gifted trio.

The Gatlins were West Texans. Larry was born in Seminole on May 2, 1948. Steven Daryl and Rudy Michael were born in Olney, Texas, on April 4, 1951, and August 20, 1952. The brothers grew up with church music, while their father, an oil driller, frequently took their family to gospel "sings."

The Gatlins admired the close harmony of the gospel groups. At church events, Larry sang the lead while his brothers harmonized behind him, and each brother would take the lead in time. Throughout boyhood, the Gatlin brothers sang at churches and on local radio and television shows. As teenagers, they recorded a religious album for an independent label.

A star athlete in high school, Larry won a football scholarship to the University of Houston. In addition, he majored in English, which aided his growing ability as a songwriter. After college, Larry joined the Imperials, a group that featured gospel music and which had backed Elvis Presley. The Imperials also worked with Jimmy Dean's Las Vegas show, and in Vegas, Larry met Dottie West. After Larry sent her a tape with eight of his original songs, Dottie responded with a plane ticket to Nashville.

In Nashville, Larry sang backup on Kris Kristofferson recordings. Dottie West recorded two of his songs, and Kristofferson also covered his material. Elvis Presley, Johnny Cash, Barbra Streisand, and Tom Jones are among the artists who would record Larry Gatlin's songs.

The Gatlin Brothers. L to R:Steve, Rudy and Larry.

While Larry was launching his music career, Steve and Rudy were earning degrees at Texas Tech. Steve took a BS in elementary education, and Rudy graduated with a BA in business administration. Steve and Rudy teamed up with their sister, LaDonna, and her husband, Tim, to form a group called Young Country. Young country toured with Tammy Wynette for a year, opening and singing backup for the country superstar.

Meanwhile, Kris Kristofferson helped Larry land a recording contract with Monument Records in 1973. Larry brought in Steve and Rudy to record with him. The debut album, *The Pilgrim*, was released early in 1974. The third album, *Larry Gatlin and Friends*, featured "Broken Lady," which won a Grammy for Best Country Song in 1976.

Other top five hits during the Monument years were "I Don't Wanna Cry," "Love is Just a Game," and "Night Time Magic." Larry reached number one for the first time in 1978 with "I Just Wish You Were Someone I Love."

The Gatlin brothers moved to Columbia Records in 1979 and became known as Larry Gatlin and the Gatlin Brothers Band. Larry played guitar, Steve handled the bass guitar, and Rudy played acoustic guitar. No harmony is as close and smooth as family harmony, and the three brothers produced beautiful vocals, with Steve providing low harmony and Rudy singing high harmony.

"All the Gold in California," a song from their first album for Columbia, soared to number one and was named Single of the Year for 1979 by the Academy of Country Music. Larry Gatlin also co-wrote his autobiography, *All the Gold in California* with Jeff Lenburg in 2003.

Another numbr one came in 1984, "Houston (Means One Day Closer to You)." Other top five hits for Columbia included "What Are We Doin' Lonesome," "Take Me to Your Lovin' Place," "Sure Feels Like Love," "She Used to Be Some-

Marty Stuart delighted the audience as a 2005 guest performer.

body's Baby," "Talkin' to the Moon," and "Love of a Lifetime."

By the mid-1980s, the Gatlins were troubled by alcohol and drugs, but counseling, willpower, and a month-long rehabilitation program for Larry straightened out their problems.

They were at the height of popularity as a close harmony group and resumed a hectic performing and recording schedule. The Gatlins were members of the *Grand Ole Opry*, and highlight performances included *The Tonight Show*, the White House, and Radio City Music Hall in New York City.

But in 1992, the Gatlin brothers decided to get off the road and spend more time with their families. So they launched the "Adios Tour," and an album, *Adios*, came out of the experience.

The Gatlins now shifted their operations to Branson, Mo., performing regularly at their own entertainment complex and periodic appearances in Las Vegas. Rudy Gatlin starred in *Oklahoma*, and *Annie Get Your Gun* in Broadway Branson USA. Larry went to New York in 1993 to take over the title role in the award-winning Broadway musical *Will Rogers Follies*.

Each of the Gatlin brothers is married with children. Larry and Janis are the parents of a son and daughter, Kristin and Josh, and now they are grandparents. Steve and Cynthia have three daughters, Ashley, Allison, and Aubrie. Rudy and Kim, married for twelve years, are the parents of Austin and Lauren.

Steve Gatlin handles interview requests for the brothers, and he schedules recording sessions. Steve has produced three Christmas CDs, and he speaks at churches.

Rudy Gatlin manages special projects, especially charitable endeavors. Most of the charity activities involve golf. All three brothers are excellent athletes who shared a passion for golf. In addition, the Gatlins frequently play in celebrity fundraiser tournaments.

Still, in great demand by audiences, the brother act that began in West Texas churches half a century ago continues to find new fans.

Ralph Emery had to attend a wedding that conflicted with the 2006 TCMHOF, but country star Jeannie Seely capably handled emcee duties. Emery would return to Carthage as emcee in 2007.

The tenth annual TCMHOF induction was conducted in 2007, with no dropoff in entertainment excitement. Fans responded warmly to Johnny Rodriguez, Red Steagall, and Bob Luman.

* * * *

Johnny Rodriguez burst onto the music scene during the 1970s as the first Chicano country artist. Today he remains the greatest and most memorable Chicano country singer of all time.

Juan Raoul Davis Rodriguez was born on December 10, 1951, in Sabinal, in South Texas. Johnny was the second youngest of ten children. The family had lived in a four-room house, and Johnny was an altar boy. When Johnny was seven, his older brother, Andres, bought him a guitar. Johnny became a fine performer, and when he was sixteen, he formed a band.

But that same year, his father died of cancer, and Andres was killed in an auto crash the next year. Although Johnny was a letterman on his high school football team, the loss of his father and brother sent him spiraling into trouble. Jailed four times by the age of eighteen, Johnny was overheard singing in his cell by famed Texas Ranger Joaquin Jackson.

Captain Jackson intervened on Johnny's behalf with Happy Shahan, who had built Alamo Village in Brackettville for John Wayne's epic motion picture, *The Alamo*. Shahan also operated Alamo Village as a popular tourist attraction and hired nineteen-year-old Rodriguez as a singer and stagecoach driver.

In 1971, Johnny's second summer at Alamo Village, his act was heard by Tom T. Hall and Bobby Bare, who were on tour in the area. Hall and Bare brought Johnny to Nashville, where he became a lead guitarist in Tom's band. Hall helped Johnny arrange a recording contract.

After his first single, "Pass Me By," reached the top ten, the Academy of Country Music voted him "Most Promising Vocalist." The promise of this award was borne out in 1973 when all three of his releases soared to number one: "You Always Come Back," "Ridin' My Thumb to Mexico," and "That's the Way Love Goes."

The following year "Dance With Me" and "We're Over" made the top three. Also, in 1974 Johnny's name was added to the Walkway of the Stars at the Country Music Hall of Fame.

A spectacular year followed when all three of

Johnny's 1975 releases again hit number one: "I Just Can't Get Her Out of Her Mind," "Just Get Up and Close the Door," and "Love Put a Song in My Heart."

Johnny's great popularity led to an acting gig in the television series *Adam 12*. He made a guest appearance on *The Dating Game* and soon became a favorite guest performer on numerous variety shows. Fans especially enjoyed his technique of using Spanish phrases while singing a familiar ballad.

Johnny was a fan favorite on personal appearance tours. Eventually, he toured all fifty states and Mexico, Canada, England, France, Germany, Belgium, Switzerland, Poland, Japan, and South Korea. He has received standing ovations at venues from Carnegie Hall to the Ryman Auditorium.

During the early 1980s, Johnny suffered se-

Tejano artist Johnny Rodriguez created a warm crowd response with his 2007 inductee performance.

vere injuries in a karate accident, problems with his vocal cords, and the personal trauma of a marriage breakup. But he struggled through these troubles and again began producing hits. He has recorded six number one hits during his career.

Johnny's lovely daughter, Aubry Rae Rodriguez, joined him on stage for the presentation of his plaque. The two of them completely won the heart of the audience, and a few years later, Johnny would be welcomed back as a guest performer.

* * * *

Like Gentleman Jim Reeves, Bob Luman was a talented baseball player as well as a smooth and gifted country artist. Also, like Gentleman Jim, Luman's career was cut short by a tragically early end.

Bobby Glenn Luman was born in Nacogdoches, Texas, on April 15, 1937. Throughout his boyhood, he was fascinated by sports and excelled as a baseball player. But music also exerted a deep appeal for Bobby Glenn. His father was an accomplished musician who taught Bobby Glenn to play several stringed instruments, including the guitar. Impressed by the country stars of the day, he modeled his singing style after his special friend, Lefty Frizzell.

The family moved to Kilgore, where Bobby Glenn became a Kilgore High School Bulldog baseball team star. The young athlete attracted the attention of pro scouts, but he could not resist the pull of music.

Attending a country music package show, Bobby Glenn was profoundly affected by the wild performance of young Elvis Presley. Girls in the audience were driven into frenzies by the gyrations and rockabilly sounds of Elvis.

"That was the last time I tried to sound like Lefty Frizell," recalled Luman.

Bobby Glenn formed a band and, strongly influenced by rockabilly, began playing at school dances and in nearby clubs. Then, after winning a talent contest, he was booked onto the Louisiana Hayride in Shreveport.

Doors opened rapidly for the handsome Texan with the rich, velvety voice. First, Bob Luman became a regular member of the Louisiana Hayride. Next, he went to Hollywood for a small part in the 1957 motion picture *Carnival Park*. Then, in Las Vegas, he performed at the Showboat Hotel on a show with Tex Ritter and Johnny Cash.

Despite these successes, a recording contract with a major label failed to produce any hits. Frustrated, Luman announced onstage at a performance that he had decided to leave country music and sign a minor league baseball contract with the Pittsburgh Pirates organization.

Fortunately, the popular Everly Brothers, Don and Phil, were in the audience. The Everly Brothers persuaded Luman to give country music one more try with "Let's Think About Living," — which sold one million copies.

But his music career was interrupted by the Selective Service, which placed him in an army uniform for two years. Soon after his discharge, Bob Luman became a popular member of the *Grand Ole Opry*. Numerous hits included "Honky Tonk Man," "Lonely Women Make Good Lovers," and "Still Loving You."

Luman was a natural for television. He appeared on the *Johnny Cash Show, Hee Haw, American Bandstand, Dean Martin's Music Country, The Bill Anderson Show, The Del Reeves Show,* and *That Good Old Nashville Music.*

The popular star toured throughout the United States, as well as in Europe and Japan. In addition, he was the first country artist to perform in San Juan, Puerto Rico.

Luman found time to marry, and Bob and Barbara had a daughter, Melissa. But Luman's heavy schedule eroded his health. He was felled by a heart attack in 1975. Although only thirty-eight, Luman spent five months recuperating at Parkland Hospital in Dallas.

Finally released, he returned to the *Grand Ole Opry*, then resumed touring and recording. But Luman contracted pneumonia, straining his weakened heart. On December 27, 1978, country music lost the forty-one-year-old star from Texas.

* * * *

Red Steagall was named "2006 Poet Laureate of Texas" in ceremonies at the State Capitol in Austin. Long referred to as the "Cowboy Poet of Texas," Red became the first cowboy poet to be appointed as the state's Poet Laureate.

This honor was the latest in a long list of impressive awards for the talented Texan. Five times through the years, Red earned the Wrangler Award for Original Music presented by the National Cowboy and Western Heritage Museum in Oklahoma City. In 2003 this prestigious institution placed Red Steagall in the Hall of Great Westerners, alongside famed cowboy artist Charles Russell, legendary cattleman Charles Goodnight, humorist Will Rogers, and rancher-Rough Rider Teddy Roosevelt.

The State Legislature honored Steagall as "The Official Cowboy Poet of Texas" in 1991.

Red Steagall was an audience favorite as a 2007 inductee.

Three years later, Red was added to the Texas Trail Hall of Fame in the Fort Worth Stockyards National Historic District. Other members of the Texas Trail of Fame include Gene Autry, Charles Goodnight, Quanah Parker, Roy Rogers, and Tex Ritter.

Russell Steagall was born on December 22, 1937, in Gainesville, Texas. The family moved to West Texas, settling in the ranching community of Sanford. Fascinated by cowboys and rodeos, Red became a bull rider as a teenager.

But when he was fifteen, he was stricken with polio. To rehabilitate his left arm and hand, Red began playing the guitar and mandolin, quickly demonstrating talent as a performer and composer.

Red enrolled at West Texas A&M, and he organized a country band to help pay college expenses. Then, graduating with a degree in animal science and agronomy, he took a job selling agrochemicals.

But at night and on weekends, he continued to perform, and in the mid-sixties, he moved to Los Angeles to focus on a music career. Red performed at clubs in the LA area and wrote songs. In 1967 Ray Charles scored a hit with Red's "Here We Go Again," which also was covered two years later by Nancy Sinatra. Through the years, more than 200 of Red's songs have been recorded by such big-name artists as Dean Martin, Roy Clark, and Johnny Duncan.

Red appeared in several motion pictures, including *Savannah Smiles*, *Drive-In*, *Benji the Hunted*, *Dark Before the Dawn*, *Shadows on the Wall*, and *Vanishing Point*. He has been seen on TV on *Hee Haw*, *Nashville on the Road*, and a host of such rodeo events as the College National Finals Rodeo and the National Finals Rodeo. He has hosted *In the Bunkhouse* on RFD-TV and *Somewhere West of Wall Street*. His one-hour radio show, *Cowboy Corner*, is broadcast over 170 stations in forty-three states.

While performing at the 1974 National Rodeo Finals in Oklahoma City, Red discovered Reba McEntire. He brought her to Nashville, introduced her to friends, and helped record her first demo tape.

Recording for Capitol in 1972, Red enjoyed a hit with "Party Dolls and Wine." His next release, "Somewhere My Love," reached the top twenty.

Red moved to Nashville in 1973. A series of hits included "Truck Drivin' Man," "Someone Cares for You," and "Lone Star Beer and Bob Wills Music," which made the top fifteen. During his career, he has recorded more than twenty albums.

Touring at least 200 days annually for more than thirty years, Red has appeared in Europe, the Far East, South America, and the Middle East. In 1983 he performed for President Reagan in the White House.

By that time, Red had moved back to Texas, headquartering in Fort Worth. Beginning in 1991, he staged the Red Steagall Cowboy Gathering and Western Swing Festival each October in the Fort Worth Stockyards.

At the 2007 TCMHOF gathering in Carthage, Red delighted the crowd — just as he has delighted and entertained countless other audiences. And like Tex Ritter and Gene Autry, Red Steagall added a strong cowboy flavor to our country and western music.

Chapter Six
The C&W Artists of 2008-2013

As the Texas Country Music Hall of Fame entered its second decade, the stars continued to cluster over Carthage each August. The class of 2008, for example, featured Buck Owens, The Whites, and acclaimed songwriter Mickey Newbury.

For many fans, the principal identity of Buck Owens is the overall-clad hillbilly who co-hosted *Hee Haw* with Roy Clark. But during the 1960s and 1970s, Buck soared to musical success and influence enjoyed by few other country stars.

Alvis Edgar Owens was born into a family of sharecroppers on August 12, 1929, in Sherman, Texas. Always called "Buck," the towheaded little boy moved with his family to Mesa, Ariz., during the Great Depression. Growing up during hard times, Buck dropped out of school in the ninth grade to work on the farm. But like many other children of the Depression, he was fiercely ambitious.

Keenly interested in music, Buck learned to play the guitar, later picking up the trumpet and saxophone. While still in his teens, he began to perform in Phoenix clubs and honky tonks, as well as on local radio. At nineteen, Buck married fellow country singer Bonnie Owens. The couple had two sons, and although Buck and Bonnie later divorced, they amicably shared the raising of their boys. Buck would marry three more times, including a final happy union with Jennifer Smith.

In 1951 Buck, Bonnie, and their sons moved to Bakersfield, Calif., where Buck performed regularly in local clubs. He spent several years playing guitar during recording sessions at Capitol Records. In 1958 Buck's cover of "Second Fiddle" reached number twenty-four on the country charts, but he had little confidence in his future as a recording artist.

In 1958 Buck moved to Tacoma, Wash., where he played clubs in the area and hosted a live radio show (one of his guests was a young Loretta Lynn). Buck met musician Don Rich, who

Buddy Owens had often performed with his father, and he represented Buck Owns at the 2008 induction ceremony with great pride and obvious pleasure.

became his partner and band member. Another band member, bassist, and future superstar Merle Haggard named Buck's band the "Buckaroos."

Late in 1959, "Under Your Spell Again" reached number four, beginning a nearly uninterrupted string of top ten hits that continued into the 1970s. The first of more than thirty albums was released in 1961. Buck's first number one single, "Act Naturally," appeared in 1963 and began fifteen consecutive number one hits, including "I've Got a Tiger By the Tail" in 1965.

Buck performed before a capacity crowd at Carnegie Hall in New York City on March 25, 1966. On tour, he commanded top concert fees, and he appeared in two motion pictures. Buck, Merle Haggard, and other artists produced the Bakersfield Sound, a hard-country honky tonk sound that contrasted with the smooth Nashville music of the era. The Bakersfield King built a state-of-the-art recording studio in the community that sometimes was called "Bakersfield."

From 1966 through 1973, the half-hour *Buck Owens Ranch TV Show* aired over as many as 100 stations. In 1969 *Hee Haw* premiered on CBS-TV and enjoyed immense popularity on the network and in syndication. Although Buck cut back on performing, in 1988, Buck and Dwight Yoakum released a duet, "Streets of Bakersfield," which was Buck's first number one since 1972.

Among a host of awards for the Bakersfield King was induction into Nashville's Country Music Hall of Fame in 1996. After suffering health problems, Buck died in his sleep in Bakersfield on March 25, 2006. Buddy Owens, Buck's oldest son, headlined the TCMHOF acceptance show.

* * * *

The Whites performed joyously for the 2008 TCMHOF audience. The group originated with the musically gifted H.S. "Buck" White. Born in 1930 in Oklahoma, Buck was raised in Wichita Falls, Texas. As a boy, he learned to play the piano, and later, he added the mandolin, guitar, banjo, fiddle, and harmonica to his performance repertoire. Forming a small band in high school, Buck increasingly focused on mandolin and piano while learning from the music of Bob Wills, Bill Monroe, and the Callahan Brothers.

With a growing reputation as an instrumentalist, Buck often was called to man the piano when such stars as Lefty Frizzell and Hank Snow performed in the area. Buck played on a radio station out of Vernon, Texas, before moving to Abilene.

While playing a show in Abilene, Buck met singer, Pat Goza. Buck and Pat married in 1950 and made their home in Abilene. Daughters Sharon and Cheryl were born in 1953 and 1955 in Abilene, where younger daughters Melissa and Rosanne were also born.

The growing White family moved to Fort Smith, Ark., in 1962. Buck and Pat teamed with Arnold and Peggy Johnston as the Down Home Folks. Four years later, Sharon, Cheryl, Teddie, and Eddie Johnston became the Down Home Kids. Sharon played guitar, and Cheryl was on bass.

In 1971 the Whites moved to Nashville, calling themselves Buck and the Down Home Folks. The following year the first of more than a dozen albums appeared, and touring schedules took the group as far as Japan. Pat retired in 1973 to focus on family life, and Sharon married bluegrass star Ricky Skaggs in 1981. Sharon and Ricky have three children. Ricky often performed with the Whites, and Rosanne White filled in while Sharon Skaggs took maternity leave.

Top ten hits for the Whites during the 1980s included "You Put the Blue in Me," "Hangin' Around," "I Wonder Who's Holding My Baby Tonight," and "Pins and Needles." Audiences always respond enthusiastically to the gospel and bluegrass numbers of The Whites.

Sharon looked back over four decades of performing with the Down Home Kids, the Buck White family, and The Whites. "There's nothing like music to bring a family together."

The Whites posed in front of their display in the TCMHOF.

* * * *

Mickey Newbury was only forty when he was voted into the Nashville Songwriters Hall of Fame. "I learned more about songwriting from Mickey than I did any other single human being," declared Kris Kristofferson, a 2007 inductee of the Texas Country Music Hall of Fame.

"To me, he was a songbird. He comes out with amazing words and music," added Kristofferson. "He was my hero and still is."

Milton Sims Newbury, Jr., was born in Houston on May 19, 1940. In high school, Mickey learned to play the guitar, formed a band, and began writing songs. He also wrote poetry, which he read in Houston to coffee house crowds. In addition, he frequented Houston's black music scene, hanging out in blues clubs, where Gate-

mouth Brown nicknamed him "The Little White Wolf." Mickey and his band performed at Texas military bases, and in 1959 he enlisted in the U.S. Air Force.

While in uniform, Mickey continued to write songs, and soon after his four-year hitch ended, he gravitated to Nashville, becoming a songwriter with Acuff-Rose Music. Mickey became friends with newcomers like Kris Kristofferson, Willie Nelson, Roger Miller, and Tom T. Hall. These gifted artists were instrumental in revolutionizing country music, introducing greater emotional depth and new musical influences.

Newbury authority Kurt Wolff stated that Mickey "infused his country music with haunting beauty and spiritual melancholy, creating an impressive collection of introspective, emo-

Singer-songwriter Mickey Newbury, who passed away in 2002, was inducted into the TCMHOF in 2008.

tionally complex songs." Over the next three decades, Mickey recorded fifteen albums in "his soft, beautiful tenor voice," although other artists would enjoy greater success on the charts with his material.

Don Gibson enjoyed a top ten country hit in 1966 with "Funny, Familiar, Forgotten Feelings," and the following year, the song became a pop hit for Tom Jones. In 1968 Mickey's boyhood friend, Kenny Rogers, scored a top five single with "Just Dropped In (To See What Condition My Condition Was In)." That same year Eddie Arnold reached the top five with "Here Comes the Rain, Baby." Another 1968 success was "Sweet Memories," recorded by Andy Williams. Dottie West and Don Gibson covered this pop hit the following year and placed "Sweet Memories" on the country chart.

Other recording artists who covered Newbury songs included Waylon Jennings, Willie Nelson, Joan Baez, Jerry Lee Lewis, Ray Charles, and the Everly Brothers. Mickey's moving arrangement of three songs, "Dixie," "Battle Hymn of the Republic," and "All My Trials," became the compilation "American Trilogy." Elvis Pres-

ley enjoyed a major hit with "American Trilogy," which became a standard in his act.

Mickey left the Nashville spotlight when he moved to Eugene, Ore., with his wife, Susan. The father of five children, Mickey continued to compose and occasionally record. But by 2002, he had contracted a lung ailment. The acclaimed songwriter died at sixty-two on September 29, 2002.

A crowd-pleasing trio of stars was inducted into the TCMHOF in 2009: Michael Martin Murphey, Neal McCoy, and Carthage's own Linda Davis.

* * * *

In the same way that Singing Cowboy Tex Ritter emphasized the western in country and western, Michael Martin Murphey — the "Singing Cowboy Poet" — writes and sings about cowboys and gunfighters. Bill O'Neal, the author of *Encyclopedia of Western Gunfighters*, had seen a reference to this book on one of Murphey's CD covers. Before Murphey's TCMHOF induction, O'Neal visited backstage to present an inscribed copy of another western topic, *Historic Ranches of the Old West*. Murphey welcomed the intrusion, genially peppered the author with questions about Wild West gunfighters and ranchers, and warmly kept up the conversation until summoned to go onstage.

Michael Martin Murphey began absorbing the cowboy culture while working on family ranches. At the Sky Ranch in Lewisville, north of Dallas, young Murphey sang cowboy songs for campfire gatherings. As a boy growing up in Dallas, he wrote cowboy poetry, and in high school, as half of the Texas Twosome, Murphey played clubs and coffee houses around the city. Attending North Texas State University, he formed a band and built a strong following around Denton and Dallas.

Murphey transferred to the University of California, Los Angeles, to study poetry and writing. Within a few months, he signed a song-writing contract with Sparrow Music and played and sang with folk bands. Then, deciding to retreat from Los Angeles to the Mojave Desert, he experienced a creative surge. He began composing songs recorded by Roger Miller, Bobbie Gentry, Flatt and Scruggs, and the Monkees.

Moving back to Texas in 1971, Murphey settled in Austin and became friends with Willie Nelson. Murphey organized a band that played at the famous Armadillo World Headquarters Club, and he signed a new contract with A&M Records.

In 1974 Murphey moved to Colorado, writing, recording, and studying the heritage of the West. His 1975 album, *Blue Sky-Night Thunder*, went gold, and a single from this album, the haunting "Wildfire," became a number three pop hit. In 1981 he wrote the screenplay for and appeared in the motion picture *Hard Country* with Kim Basinger and Jan-Michael Vincent.

In 1982 "What's Forever For" became his first number one country hit, and the following year he was named Best New Male Vocalist by the Academy of Country Music. There were numerous other hits, and in 1987 he returned to number one with "A Long Line of Love." During the 1990s, Murphey staged a three-day WestFest, a festival celebrating Western Americana, at locations in Texas, Colorado, and New Mexico.

Murphey's 1990 album, *Cowboy Songs*, went gold and earned the first of his six Wrangler Awards from the National Cowboy Hall of Fame. *Cowboy Christmas* and *Cowboy Songs II* were released the following year, and *Cowboy Songs III* was produced in 1993. Two years later, Murphey, performing with the San Antonio Symphony Orchestra, released *Sagebrush Symphony*. *Cowboy Songs IV* and *Cowboy Christmas II* and *III* have followed, along with other popular albums, including *Tall Grass & Cool Water* in 2012 and *Red River Drifter* the following year.

There was a special gig in 2011 at Ralph Lau-

Michael Martin Murphey has focused his immense talents on creating and presenting cowboy music, and in addition to numerous musical honors he has received six Wrangler Awards from the National Cowboy Hall of Fame.

ren's Double R.L. Ranch near Ridgway, Colo., where Murphey had visited for three decades. "I go there to write songs from time to time," said Murphey. "It's the most spectacular ranch in the Rockies."

On September 4, Murphey was at the ranch to perform at the wedding of his friend David Lauren and Laura Bush, niece of former President George W. Bush. Murphey and his Rio Grande Band played "Vanishing Breed" for the couple's first dance, then performed for nearly six hours for the families and guests.

In 2019 Murphey won his most recent Wrangler Award for his induction into the Cowboy Hall of Fame at the National Cowboy and Western Heritage Awards. His numerous other honors include induction into the Texas Country Music Hall of Fame, where he was a massive hit with a laughing, cheering crowd.

* * * *

"Linda Davis is absolutely one of the best singers in the business." This accolade came from country superstar Kenny Rogers. "In this business, there are people who can sing, and there are singers," explained Rogers. "She is the best."

Grammy-winning singer Linda Davis is a Panola County native who began her performing career as a child. Born in the rural community of Dotson, Linda was singing in church by age six. She performed on the Gary Jamboree and, later, the Louisiana Hayride.

The popular blonde beauty was a cheerleader at Carthage High School and sang in the CHS choir. At Panola College in Carthage, Linda was a choir member and performed in The Pipers, a singing and dancing group that toured for the college. Utilizing her singing gifts in the talent contest, Linda was voted Miss Panola County as part of the Miss Texas Pageant.

In 1982, at the age of twenty, Linda moved to Nashville to pursue a career in country music. She sang in piano bars and recorded ad jingles for Dr Pepper and Kentucky Fried Chicken. With male/female duos popular, Linda and Skip Eaton performed and recorded as "Skip and Linda," scoring three minor hits in 1982.

In later years, as a solo artist, she recorded a few more marginal hits. But a breakthrough proved elusive despite Linda's popularity with everyone in the business in Nashville.

"'Emotionally, it was like a rollercoaster," recalled Linda. "We would just get on a little wave, and I'd think, 'Okay, this is going to do it.' Then it would peter out, and we'd sit there, scratch our heads, and go, why didn't this work out?"

Finally, in 1989, Linda caught the attention of another superstar, Reba McEntire.

"I was listening to songs for my next album," reminisced McEntire. "I kept hearing this particular female vocalist on the demos that blew me away. It had been a long time since a voice had moved me that way, and I just had to find out who she was."

Reba enlisted Linda Davis for her tour show.

Beautiful Linda Davis, a Grammy-winning singer from Carthage, has been a frequent presence during induction weekends either as emcee of Friday night events or as a performer during induction ceremonies. Linda was inducted into the TCMHOF in 2009.

In 1993, Reba and Linda recorded "Does He Love You" and filmed a dramatic video version of the song.

"Does He Love You" soared to number one and earned Reba and Linda the 1993 Grammy Award for the Best Country Vocal Collaboration. Linda's 1996 single, "Some Things Are Meant to Be," rose to number thirteen on the country charts.

Linda and her husband, country singer Lang Scott, are the parents of Hillary Scott. Following in her mother's footsteps, Hillary is the lead singer in the popular group Lady A.

A highlight of Linda's stage show comes when she selects a young fan from the audience to perform with her the torchy duet, "Does He Love You."

Linda earned two more Grammy Awards in 2017 for Best Contemporary Christian Album and Best Contemporary Christian Performance. Year after year, she returns to Carthage to assist with the TCMHOF induction weekend, performing onstage as a guest performer and emceeing associated events. "Whatever you need," she tells Tommie Ritter Smith. And whenever she appears, she is welcomed enthusiastically by her legion of Linda Davis fans.

* * * *

Dynamic. Exciting. Lively. Crowd Pleaser.

These words describe the electrifying stage presence of a born entertainer. Neal McCoy entered the world at Jacksonville, Texas, on July 30, 1958. His actual birth name was Hubert Neal McGaughey, Jr. Early in his performing career, Neal simplified the spelling of his last name to McGoy (same pronunciation), and there was a later change to McCoy.

As a schoolboy, Neal eagerly performed at any opportunity in school programs and musicals, church choirs, and gospel quartets. In addition to country and gospel, he absorbed elements of jazz and rock.

After high school, McCoy began playing the

Neal McCoy from Jacksonville and Longview has won a place with TCMHOF fans with his delightful stints as emcee, and, in 2009, a Hall of Fame inductee.

Texas honky tonk circuit. He won a nightclub talent contest hosted by Janie Fricke, who at that time was the opening act for Charley Pride. Janie introduced McCoy to Charley Pride's agent. When she departed to pursue a solo career, Neal McCoy became Charley Pride's opening act.

Married in 1980, Neal and Melinda McCoy made their home in Longview. Neal and Melinda have a son and a daughter.

Onstage McCoy delivers a high-energy, nonstop performance that makes him a crowd favorite. For seven years, he toured with Charley Pride, performing in almost every state in the U.S., along with Canada, England, Australia, and New Zealand.

With broad touring experience and a growing fan base, McCoy finally left the Pride tour to build his own solo career. His first album, *At This Moment*, was released in 1991, and the following year *Where Forever Begins* became his second album. His third album, 1994's *No Doubt About It*, produced his first two number one hits, the title song and "Wink." The title of his next album — *Neal McCoy* — attested to his growing fame and recognition.

In 1997 "Then You Can Tell Me Goodbye" was named Video of the Year at the TNN/Music City News Country Awards. For the next two years, 1998 and 1999, McCoy earned Entertainer of the Year honors.

"I like to entertain and have a good time with the folks," asserts McCoy. Three platinum albums, one gold album, and a sensational performing career proclaim the truth of this statement.

Neal McCoy frequently has emceed TCMHOF activities, and his rollicking interaction with audience members creates uproarious hilarity. As a result, he was welcomed warmly into the TCMHOF (he jokingly calls it "the Neal McCoy Hall of Fame"), and his subsequent appearances have generated a gleeful fan response.

* * * *

Chester Stout, whose health failed in his late eighties, died in 2010. A plaque in the TCMHOF notes the "generous contributions by Chester Stout in memory of his beloved wife."

Referring to the Texas Country Music Hall of Fame, Stout stated that "I sincerely believe that it has been one of the most significant happenings that has occurred . . . in recent years." Stout expressed his hope "that my gift to the museum will be appreciated and this community project will be supported by the citizens of Panola County, country music fans and the businesses who will benefit." Chester Stout's hope was fulfilled every August.

* * * *

In August 2010, two thousand country music fans crowded into the Carthage Community Center for the induction of George Jones, Al Dexter, and Ray Winkler. The popular Mel Tillis and his Statesiders were present to lead the cast of guest performers. Indeed, there was a list of five hundred fans who wanted tickets, if any became available.

The famed country artist nicknamed "Ol' Possum" also is known within the industry as the "Rolls Royce of Country Singers." Gary Hartman, the author of *The History of Texas Music*, states that George Jones "is famous for his unique vocal style, which features an emotional depth and resonance rarely matched by other country singers."

The country roots of George Jones run deep. He was born in a rural log cabin near Saratoga, Texas, on September 12, 1931. His father played guitar, his mother was a pianist, and George was given a guitar when he was nine. The boy liked church music but soon was drawn to country sounds.

As a teenager, George performed on radio stations in Jasper and Beaumont. He married at 19, divorced a year later, then enlisted in the Marine Corps. Stationed in California, Jones played and sang in bars when he was off-duty.

Following his discharge in 1953, George returned to Texas. He soon began a stellar recording career that has produced thirteen number one hits, thirty top five songs, and scores of other recordings that have placed high on the country charts. His first hit came in 1955, "Why Baby Why," which he co-wrote.

That year he joined the Louisiana Hayride in Shreveport, co-billing with young Elvis Presley. In 1956 he was invited to join the cast of the *Grand Ole Opry*, and later that year, the first of nearly ninety albums appeared.

His first number one was "White Lightning,"

released in 1959 and crossed over to the pop charts. Other classic hits included "The Race Is On," "She Thinks I Still Care," "He Stopped Loving Her Today," and a parade of others.

Along with his parade of hits, George Jones earned a parade of awards. In 1956 he was voted Most Promising New Country Vocalist. He was named Male Vocalist of the Year in 1962, 1963, 1980, and 1981 by multiple groups, such as CMA, *Cash Box*, and *Billboard*. He won a Grammy in 1980 for "He Stopped Loving Her Today," and in 1992, Ol' Possum was elected to Nashville's Country Music Hall of Fame.

Among a host of other awards were Top Vocal Duo wins in 1972, 1973, and 1976, all with Tammy Wynette.

George married Tammy in 1968. In 1973 their duet, "We're Gonna Hold On," Went to number one, and in 1976 they had two number one hits, "Golden Ring" and "Near You." They enjoyed many other duet hits, but George was spiraling out of control.

In one year, he missed fity-four dates and was called "No Show" Jones for a few years. After that, his weight dropped from 150 to 100 pounds. But in 1983, he married Nancy Sepulvado, who helped him regain his health and his Hall of Fame career.

"His voice was like a Stradivarius violin," proclaimed Merle Haggard in *Rolling Stone*, "one of the greatest instruments ever made." David Hadju stated in the *New Republic*, "George Jones ranks with Frank Sinatra and Billie Holliday." Emmylou Harris declared that "when you hear George Jones sing, you are hearing a man who takes a song and makes it a work of art — always."

Jones had a superb gift for harmony. There were numerous memorable duets with Tammy Wynette, as well as more than sixty recorded pairings with artists from Loretta Lynn to Jerry Lee Lewis, Buck Owens to Lynn Anderson, Waylon Jennings to Brenda Lee, Ricky Skaggs to Charlie Daniels, B.B. King to Randy Travis, Ernest Tubb to Johnny Cash, Willie Nelson to Dolly Parton.

One of the greatest stars ever to grace the TCMHOF stage was 2010 inductee George Jones. "His voice was like a Stradivarius violin," proclaimed Merle Haggard.

In 2012 George Jones received the Grammy Lifetime Achievement Award. But by that time, he was suffering a serious respiratory ailment. In August 2012, he announced a farewell tour, with performances in sixty cities. Following a concert in Knoxville, Tenn., he was hospitalized, and after several days in intensive care, the eighty-one-year-old singer died.

* * * *

"How would you talk to a woman with a gun?" mused Al Dexter after seeing a gun-toting waitress give chase to her husband's girlfriend, "and I thought, 'lay that pistol down, babe, lay that pistol down.'"

With this incident and lyric phase in mind, songwriter-musician Al Dexter created "Pistol Packin' Mama," one of the biggest honky tonk hits of all time. Dexter already was an experienced performing and recording artist, and "Pistol Packin' Mama" launched five years of phenomenal success for the East Texan.

Clarence Albert Poindexter was born on May 4, 1902, in Jacksonville, Texas. As a boy, he became an adept musician, learning to play the guitar, banjo, organ, fiddle, and mouth harp while singing and writing songs. Beginning with local parties and barn dances during the 1920s, he moved to dance halls in Longview during the oil boom of the 1930s.

Along the way, he shortened his name to "Al Dexter." Dexter formed a band, the Texas Troopers, and opened the Round-Up Club at Turnertown, located in the midst of the booming East Texas Oil Field. Al and his Texas Troopers began recording in 1934, often his own compositions. In 1937 he introduced the term "honky tonk" with his song "Honky Tonk Blues."

At his own honky tonk tavern, he witnessed one of his waitresses produce a pistol and chase her husband's girlfriend through a barbed wire fence. Al recorded "Pistol Packin' Mama" in 1943, and during the next twenty-two months, it sold three million singles and 200,000 copies of the sheet music. Bing Crosby and the Andrews Sisters scored a hit with the catchy tune many other artists covered. By 1944 "Pistol Packin' Mama" had crossed over to the top of the pop charts.

In 1944 Al and the Texas Troopers hit number one with "Rosalita." The following year "I'm Losing My Mind Over You" spent seven weeks atop the country charts. In 1946 Al moved from the OKeh label to Columbia Records. "Guitar Polka" was number one for sixteen weeks and crossed over to the pop charts, while "Wine,

Al Dexter attained musical popularity in the honky-tonks of the East Texas Oil Field, and his widow proudly accepted his TCM-HOF plaque.

Women and Song" topped the country charts for five weeks.

During 1943-1948 Al Dexter received twelve gold records for million sellers; in 1946, he was voted Leading Artist by the Jukebox Operators of America. Lefty Frizzell and Merle Haggard were among the young artists influenced by Al and his honky tonk style.

Al opened the Bridgeport Club in Dallas, where he performed until he retired. In 1971 he was inducted into the Nashville Songwriters Hall of Fame.

Al's first composition was "Going Home to Glory," which he did at eighty-one on January

28, 1984. His family was most excited at Al's admission to the TCMHOF and made a great deal of memorabilia available to the museum.

* * * *

Ray Winkler eagerly looked forward to the Texas Country Music Hall of Fame inaugural induction show in August 1998, which would honor his dear friend, Jim Reeves, and had given his blessing for the opening notes of "Welcome To My World" to be used in the logo. But unfortunately, his attendance was not to be, as he passed away in May 1998.

In collaboration with John Hathcock, Winkler wrote: "Welcome to My World" for Reeves in 1961. Winkler and Hathcock wrote hundreds of songs together, and many have been recorded. But "Welcome To My World" was their masterpiece, a classic that would be recorded by more than 140 artists and a standard that would provide definition for Jim Reeves.

Rayburn Franklin Winkler was born in Bonham, Texas, on October 13, 1920. After high school, he moved to Dallas to pursue a business education and a career in radio broadcasting. In 1942 he married the love of his life, Libby Carmical, and soon entered the U.S. Navy, working as a recruiter and on a public radio show in Little Rock, Ark..

After World War II, Winkler moved to sports broadcasting and announced professional league baseball games. He then had an opportunity to become general manager of the Lubbock Hubbers and became president of the West Texas-New Mexico Pro Baseball League.

In 1955, Ray was fortunate to get back into radio with ownership of a new radio station KZIP in Amarillo. John Hathcock came to work at KZIP, sharing a gift for songwriting with Winkler.

One regular visitor of KZIP was Jim Reeves. Like many other country artists, Jim stopped by KZIP when in Amarillo for personal appearances. As a former disk jockey and minor league baseball player, he had much in common with Ray Winkler.

Ray had hoped to write a song for Gentleman Jim, and he and Hathcock tested songs on Reeves every time he appeared in Amarillo. "You're getting better," responded Reeves.

Reeves liked the sound of "Welcome To My World," with lyrics by Winkler and music by Hathcock. Jim took the original demo by Dean Kelley to sing it on his tour bus, while playing golf, and even while getting a hair-

Mel Tillis and his band, the Statesiders, provided a rousing guest performance at the 2010 induction.

Ray Winkler from Bonham was a busy radio broadcaster and songwriter who composed "Welcome to My World" for his friend, Jim Reeves. His TCMHOF plaque was accepted by his daughter, Betty Winkler Hodges, who stands with Ray's longtime friend and collaborator, deejay Dean Kelley.

cut. Gentleman Jim released the first recording in 1962. Immediately popular with the public, "Welcome To My World" became a mainstay of Jim's live performances.

Other artists found it irresistible. Elvis Presley, Dean Martin, Mel Tillis, Ray Price, Eddy Arnold, and more than 135 other performers covered the song, and tourists to Graceland are welcomed at the entrance with Elvis' version. In addition, it has been used in movies, television shows, commercials, plays, and countless ringtones. Most recent recordings include Raul Malo, Steve Wariner, and several Thomson Travel commercials in London showcasing the original recording by Jim Reeves.

But "Welcome To My World" belongs first and foremost to Gentleman Jim Reeves, which was the original intention of the composers. Ray

fondly wrote and recorded a recitation entitled "My Tribute To Jim Reeves," which depicts the life of his dear friend.

* * * *

In 2011 only two inductees were nominated to the TCMHOF, but both artists — Mickey Gilley and Moe Bandy — enjoyed remarkable careers. And in the early 1990s, both Mickey and Moe moved their operations to theaters in Branson, Mo.

"Room Full of Roses." "Stand By Me." "City Lights." "She's Pulling Me Back Again." "Lonely Nights." "You've Really Got a Hold on Me." "Don't the Girls All Get Prettier at Closing Time."

All of these memorable songs and many more were number one hits for Mickey Gilley. Between 1974 and 1983, Gilley recorded seventeen number one releases, including six in a row in 1980 and 1981. Several of these hits crossed over to the pop charts, making Mickey a leader of the "Countrypolitan" genre. And throughout this period of superstardom, the award-winning pianist-singer presided over "The World's Biggest Honky Tonk," Gilley's in Pasadena, Texas.

Mickey Leroy Gilley was born on March 9, 1936, in Natchez, Miss.. The family home was across the Mississippi River in nearby Ferriday, La. Mickey grew up playing the piano with his cousins Jerry Lee Lewis and Jimmy Swaggart. The three cousins played boogie woogie in high school and gospel music at Ferriday's Assembly of God Church.

At seventeen, Mickey left school to move to Houston and find construction work. But when his cousin, Jerry Lee Lewis, scored a hit with his first recording, "Crazy Arms," Mickey decided to pursue a music career. So he made a few recordings, played clubs in Louisiana and Mississippi, and returned to Houston for construction jobs.

In the early 1960s, Gilley began performing regularly at a Houston club. He built an enthusiastic local following, and in 1970, he opened Gil-

In 2011 Mickey Gilley recounted his fabled career to a captivated TCMHOF audience.

ley's Club in Pasadena with a partner. Gilley's became enormously popular, and in 1974 Mickey recorded his first number one, "Room Full of Roses." The Academy of Country Music voted Mickey Most Promising Vocalist, and as one hit followed, another *Billboard* named him Top New Country Artist in 1975.

The following year ACM chose "Don't The Girls All Get Prettier at Closing Time" as Song of the Year, while Gilley was named Male Vocalist of the Year and Entertainer of the Year.

In 1979 The World's Biggest Honky Tonk was designated ACM's Nightclub of the Year, an honor repeated in 1981, 1983, and 1984. An *Esquire* magazine article about Gilley's led to a Hollywood script and the 1980 movie *Urban Cowboy*, starring John Travolta and Debra Winger — and Gilley's mechanical bull. Mickey himself made

an onscreen appearance, and *Urban Cowboy* triggered a nationwide pop culture craze.

Mickey was given cameo roles in such television series as *Dukes of Hazzard*, *Murder She Wrote*, *Fall Guy*, and *Fantasy Island*. In 1984 he was awarded a Star on the Hollywood Walk of Fame.

In 1990 Gilley's Club burned. Soon Mickey became one of the first country performers to build a theater in Branson, giving new life to his fabled career. Gilley was awarded a star on the Hollywood Walk of Fame for his contributions to the recording industry. Unfortunately, in 2009 he was seriously injured while helping a neighbor move furniture. For a time, Mickey was paralyzed from the neck down. Physical therapy helped him return to the stage the following year, although he no longer has the hand coordination to play the piano. to play the piano. Sadly, Mickey passed away in Branson in 2022 at the age of 86."

* * * *

"If I'd done all the things I sing about, I'd be dead."

Moe Bandy achieved stardom in the 1970s and 1980s by singing about cheatin' and drinkin' and other hardcore country subjects.

His first hit, which charted number seventeen in 1974, was "I Just Started Hatin' Cheatin' Songs Today," followed quickly by "Honky Tonk Amnesia," "It Was Always So Easy (To Find an Unhappy Woman)," and "Don't Anyone Make Love at Home Anymore."

In 1975 "Hank Williams, You Wrote My Life" soared to number two. The following year, Moe scored number eleven with "Here I Am Drunk Again." A 1978 duet with Jamie Fricke, "It's a Cheating Situation," reached number one, and so did a 1979 solo, "I Cheated Me Right Out of You."

"She's Not Really Cheatin' (She's just Gettin' Even)" reached number two in 1982. Other hard country hits included "It Took a Lot of Drinkin'

(To Get That Woman Over Me)" and "Barroom Roses."

These and similar songs celebrated the rowdy lifestyle that Moe happily sang about but largely avoided himself.

"I really think my songs are about life," he explained. "There's cheating, drinking, and divorcing everywhere, and that's what hardcore country music is all about."

Marion Franklin Bandy, Jr. was born on February 12, 1944, in Meridian, Miss., the hometown of the legendary Jimmie Rodgers. The little boy was nicknamed "Moe" by his father, who moved his family to San Antonio in 1950.

Moe Bandy was a charming and grateful 2011 recipient who posed with Tommie Ritter Smith and his TCMHOF plaque.

His father taught Moe to play the guitar, and his mother played piano and sang. Moe occasionally played with his father's band, the Mission City Playboys.

But Moe's greatest interest as a teenager was rodeo. He was a bronc and bull rider and rodeoed all over Texas. Moe's brother Mike was a six-time National Finals Rodeo bull riding qualifier, and in 2007 the Bandy brothers were inducted into the Texas Rodeo Cowboy Hall of Fame.

Moe's bruises and broken bones added up, however, and at eighteen, he left rodeo and formed a country band, Moe and the Mavericks. He played throughout the San Antonio area and, with the Mavericks, backed such performers as Loretta Lynn and Bob Wills.

Moe married and raised three children, and for twelve years, he toiled as a sheet metal worker during the day to make ends meet. Finally, he borrowed money to finance recording sessions, and in 1973 Moe began to score hits. By the late

1970s, he was a country chart regular.

In 1979 Bandy teamed with Joe Stampley to form the Good Ol' Boys, Moe and Joe. Immensely popular, Moe and Joe were named Duo of the Year in 1980 and 1981 by the Academy of Country Music. Moe and Joe recorded seven albums, while Moe has released thirty-five solo albums during his career.

Moe opened the Moe Bandy Americana Theatre in 1991 in Branson, Mo. Before his TCMHOF induction, Tommie Ritter Smith and her husband Bill visited Moe at a Branson performance, presented him with a Hall of Fame jacket on stage, and announced his upcoming ceremony. While there, Tommie and Bill picked up memorabilia for the museum.

Tommie and Bill visited Branson twice per year, maintaining friendships in the country music industry. On one occasion, there was an onstage visit with Mickey Gilley, which included the presentation of a TCMHOF jacket and announcing the star's upcoming induction. Such presentations provided free publicity for the Texas Country Music Hall of Fame and goodwill from the stars.

Tommie, in earlier years, had danced at Gilley's, and she pointed out to Mickey — with an obvious reference to one of his biggest hits: "The boys also get prettier at closing time." Gilley laughed, and the audience roared its delight.

New construction commenced at the Texas Country Music Hall of Fame in 2012. Since the original certificates had been paid down steadily, financing proved easy to obtain. And the same Longview construction company was engaged, in effect, to continue the project they had begun a decade earlier. But unfortunately, needed expansion took the form of a significant addition to the rear, and the museum had to be closed temporarily.

As a result, there was no induction in 2012 or 2013. But in both years, the TCMHOF put on a concert featuring numerous guest artists. These lively shows were well attended, and fans could look forward to a bigger museum and new and exciting inductees in 2014.

Chapter Seven
The Hall of Famers of 2014-2016

A star-studded period for the TCMHOF began with the induction of Duane Allen in 2014. Duane is from a rural community in northeast Texas, and he is a 1966 graduate of East Texas State University (ETSU now is known as Texas A&M University-Commerce.) Duane had extensive music training, and during the 1960s, he joined the Oak Ridge Boys. On the evening of his induction into the Texas Country Music Hall of Fame, the other members of the famous group were declared honorary Inductees into the TCMHOF. Of course, the members of the Oak Ridge Boys deserve any honor that can be bestowed.

"Elvira."

"Y'all Come Back, Saloon."

"Bobbie Sue."

"You're the One."

"Fancy-Free."

"American Made."

These and other sensational hits established the Oak Ridge Boys as one of the most famous and accomplished groups in the history of country music. This notable group had its origin in 1945 in Oak Ridge, Tenn.. Oak Ridge was a key location for researching and developing the atomic bomb during World War II. There were 75,000 men and women at Oak Ridge working on this top secret "Manhattan Project," and movies and live entertainment were brought into this confined community.

Gospel music was popular in Oak Ridge, and one of the acts began to call themselves the Oak Ridge Quartet. In 1961 the gospel group changed its name to the Oak Ridge Boys. Baritone William Lee Golden, from rural Alabama, joined the quartet in 1964, and the next year Texan Duane Allen became a member. During the early 1970s, Golden and Allen were joined by tenor Joe Bonsall from Philadelphia and by bass Richard Sterban, a New Jersey native.

With this core lineup — Allen, Golden, Bonsall, and Sterban — the Oak Ridge Boys became a top gospel group. But in 1977, producer Jim Halsey convinced them that the Oak Ridge Boys could reach a far larger audience with country music. So Halsey booked them into a Las Vegas

Duane Allen, from rural Lamar County near Paris, became a prominent member of the Oak Ridge Boys during the 1960s.

revue, where they performed seventy-percent country songs and thirty-percent gospel.

In 1977 the hit singles "Y'all Come Back Saloon" and "You're the One" vaulted the Oaks to prominence in country music. During the next eight years, the Oak Ridge Boys had twenty-five consecutive top ten singles, including thirteen number one hits. Album after album sold one million, two million copies. The Oak Ridge Boys scored their biggest hits in 1981 with "Elvira." Number one in the country charts, "Elvira" was a crossover number one in the pop charts.

The Oak Ridge Boys have earned five Grammy Awards, four Country Music Awards, two Academy of Country Music Awards, and eight Gospel Music Association Dove Awards. These honors ranged from Vocal Group of the Year to Single of the Year to Album of the Year.

"I've always believed in the philosophy that any two, three, or four can be bigger or better than anyone," states lead singer Duane Allen.

Duane is from rural Taylortown in Lamar County. He attended Paris Junior College and earned a music degree from Texas A&M University-Commerce. He received a distinguished alumni award from both institutions, and he was awarded an honorary doctorate from a Christian college. An antique car buff, he has more than two dozen classics in his museum, Ace on Wheels.

Baritone William Lee Golden was presented a lifetime achievement award from the Alabama Music Hall of Fame. A gifted painter, he created the William Lee Golden Collection.

"I go out there and try to sing the best I can and give them physically and mentally every single thing I've got."

In addition to being a high-energy performer,

Although Duane Allen is the only member of the Oak Ridge Boys who is a native Texan, the other three Oaks were declared honorary members of the TCMHOF and presented their own plaques. L to R: Joe Bonsall, Duane Allen, William Lee Golden, Richard Sterban.

tenor Joe Bonsall is a songwriter and the author of inspirational and children's books.

Bass Richard Sterban, for years, was part-owner of the Nashville Sounds Triple-A baseball club. He stores a bicycle in a bay beneath the tour bus, carries a bike in a case on plane trips, and takes long-distance rides to stay fit on the road.

"I wanted to be in the best vocal group in the world," said Sterban about his goal in life.

Fans of the Oak Ridge Boys would agree that he achieved that goal.

Audience members at the TCMHOF induction certainly agreed that he reached his goal. Indeed, fans of the Oak Ridge Boys are elated that this incomparable group continues to make 150 or more personal appearances each year.

* * * *

In 2014 Neal McCoy enlivened the TCMHOF crowd with his comedic emcee talents. In addition, there was a special group of guest performers — "Next Generation" Georgette Jones (daughter of George Jones and Tammy Wynette); Shelly West (daughter of Dotty West); Robyn Young (son of Faron Young); Rylee Scott (daughter of Linda Davis and Lang Scott); Jett Williams (daughter of Hank Williams); Hawkshaw Hawkins, Jr. (son of Hawkshaw Hawkins and Jean Shepherd); Melissa Luman (daughter of Bob Luman); and George Hamilton V (son of George Hamilton IV).

* * * *

Dallas Wayne, a noted disc jockey and veteran country performer was inducted into the disc jockey wing of the TCMHOF. A decade earlier, Dallas brought his talents to KHYI 95.9 FM in Dallas, Texas. Only a couple of years later, in 2006, the Academy of Western Artists presented him with a Will Rogers Award of Classic Country Major Market DJ of the Year.

The following year Dallas Wayne moved to SIRIUS XM Satellite Radio, where he broadcast

Neal McCoy enlivened the 2014 celebration with his rollicking humor and interaction with a delighted audience.

on Outlaw Country and at Willie's Roadhouse, the Texas-based honky-tonk channel. In 2009 Dallas was awarded a second Will Rogers Award for DJ of the Year.

Dallas Wayne performs as part of the honky-tonk group Haybale. In 2018 and 2021, he returned to Carthage as emcee of the Texas Country Music Hall of Fame Induction ceremony. Over the airwaves, he is an enthusiastic ambassador of the TCMHOF.

* * * *

Tracy Byrd was deeply honored to be inducted into the Texas Country Music Hall of Fame in 2015.

I'd never been in a studio until I cut a record and got a record deal," reflected Tracy Byrd about the course of his career. "I was a live performer. That's what I am and where I came from, and what I still love to do."

Life as a country music performer was far from the mind of young Tracy Byrd as he grew up in Vidor, Texas. When he was a little boy, his grandmother began taking him fishing, and when he was six, she bought him his first shotgun. Tracy's love for the outdoors has persisted throughout his life. Indeed, his passion for hunting and fishing and widespread popularity as a performer have placed him today as a host of two shows on the Outdoor Channel.

As a youngster, Tracy learned to play the guitar and enjoyed singing, but shyness kept him from performing. Instead, he pursued college coursework at Southwest Texas State (now Texas State University) in San Marcos and nearby Lamar University in Beaumont. But when he sang "Your Cheatin' Heart" at a shopping mall "recording studio," the manager was impressed and persuaded Tracy to perform at a local talent show. He was so impressive playing and singing "Folsom Prison Blues" and "Weary Blues From Waiting" that he received a standing ovation. The enthusiastic applause was decisive.

"All of a sudden, they couldn't get me off," he laughed. "That's all I wanted to do."

Tracy soon caught on with Beaumont native Mark Chesnutt, who was headlining at Cutters nightclub in Beaumont. Chesnutt began touring as his star rose, where Tracy Byrd formed his own band and starred at Cutters. Within a year, Byrd explored Nashville, and on his second trip in 1992, he signed with MCA and recorded an album, *Tracy Byrd*.

Tracy Byrd of Vidor and Beaumont was a crowd-pleasing inductee in 2015.

His second album, *No Ordinary Man*, was released to wide acclaim in 1993. Several singles from these albums charted, including "Holdin' Heaven," which reached number one. *Tracy Bird* was certified gold, *No Ordinary Man* was certified double platinum, and his next three albums all reached gold status. A 2019 album, *Tracy Byrd: Live at Billy Bob's Texas*, includes nineteen songs, and the dvd version has several interviews with Tracy.

Byrd promptly began touring, determined to build a fan base. "We toured from day one and never stopped," he explained. "We worked. Building a fan base like that in an old-fashioned grassroots kind of way has really been a big reason for us staying around."

Another reason has been Tracy's versatility in turning his rich voice and expressive phrasing to different styles. "I've been versatile, and I've not been trying to conform to any other thing."

From a shy youngster, Tracy Byrd has become a consummate, highly popular entertainer. "The payoff was and always will be that couple of hours on stage every night. I still love making live music and working with my band. I still love working up a show and rehearsing." He rehearses with his band, the Byrd Dawgs, organized in 2014.

Tracy and his wife, Michelle, make their home in Beaumont with two sons and a daugh-

In 2016 the TCMHOF was honored to present in concert Clint Black, the sole inductee of the year.

ter. Tracy is a devoted family man who is active in charity events. "But I feel I still have a lot to offer in music."

So do his fans.

* * * *

The Texas Country Music Hall of Fame presented a performance promontory in 2016. Tommie Ritter Smith secured Clint Black for August 2016. This outstanding country singer would be the lone inductee, and fans would enjoy the songs of a true artist. In addition, the Carthage Civic Center would stretch its seating capacity to 2,200.

"I really don't want to conform to what other people think I should be doing with my music," explains country superstar Clint Black. "Instead, I'll take my chances just being me."

By "just being me," Clint Black has sold more than twenty million albums worldwide, including thirty-one top ten hits and twenty-two number one hits.

The future award-winning singer-songwriter was born in 1962 and raised in Katy, a suburb of Houston. In his early teens, Clint taught himself to play the guitar, harmonica, and bass, and he joined his older brother, Kevin's band. Later Clint performed for several years on the Houston nightclub circuit while exercising his considerable gifts as a successful songwriter.

By late 1988 Clint had a contract with RCA Nashville. Early the next year, his first single, "A Better Man," soared to number one. Clint Black was the first new male country artist in fifteen years to have a number one hit with his debut single. His first album, *Killin' Time*, soon followed and sold two million copies. Every song on the album was entirely or at least partially written by Black, and five straight singles from the album reached number one. By the end of 1989, Clint Black was showered with awards for Best Male Vocalist, Best New Male Vocalist, and Songwriter/Artist of the Year.

Black began to make television appearances in various capacities, and his television roles have continued on occasion through the current season. In 1996 he became only the fourth country music singer to earn a star on the Hollywood Walk of Fame. Clint married fellow Houstonian and successful actress Lisa Hartman in 1991. Their daughter Lily Pearl Black was born in 2001, and Clint put his career on hold for three years to be with his daughter. Clint allowed that if the sabbatical was not the best career move, "it was a real smart dad move."

Lisa Hartman Black, a beautiful actress, also recorded songs. In 1999 she and Clint recorded a duet, "When I Say I Do," that reached number one and was nominated for a Grammy Award. Indeed, during this period, Clint Black enjoyed numerous hits, most of his own composition.

"To me, a song is more than just something to learn from," he reflected. "It's somebody else's true feeling. I'm always trying to get at the meaning."

In 2017 the TCMHOF presented Country superstar Kenny Rogers from Houston. Kenny enjoyed enormous success with his recordings that have sold 100 million copies, as well as starred in a series of TV movies.

For Clint Black fans, the star finds the true feeling in one hit after another.

* * * *

It was difficult to imagine how the TCMHOF could match the superstar 2016 appearance of Clint Black in 2017. Then, however, Tommie Ritter Smith lined up another superlative performer, Kenny Rogers, then added to the 2017 inductee list Bobbie Lee Nelson, the immensely talented pianist who also was the sister and life-long collaborator of Willie Nelson. As a result, TCMHOF fans from Carthage, Nashville, and elsewhere realized they were in for an immeasurable treat in August 2017.

Kenny Rogers was a superstar who had enjoyed a spectacular performing career as an award-winning singer and a popular actor. One of the best-selling musical artists of all time, Kenny has sold more than 165 million records worldwide while releasing over 120 hit singles and seventy albums. One of his hits, "The Gambler," led to five television movies, with Kenny in the title role. In addition, he starred in several other television movies, such as *The Dream Makers* and *Coward of the County*, as well as the 1982 motion picture, *Six Pack*.

The list of his music awards is staggering. He has won three Grammys as a performer. He was inducted into the Country Music Hall of Fame in 2013. He has earned seven awards from the Academy of Country Music, thirteen American Music Awards, and six Country Music Association Awards, including the Willie Nelson Lifetime Achievement Award in 2013. Three CMT Awards included sixth place for "Ruby Don't Take Your Love to Town" on CMT's 100 Greatest Cheating Songs.

His remarkable success was no accident. "I really studied the music business, and I realized there's only two ways to compete. You can do what everybody else is doing and do it better — and I didn't like my chances — or you could do something nobody is doing, and you don't invite comparison. I did something different, and I was lucky it was successful."

Kenneth Donald Rogers was born in 1938 in Houston. The fourth of eight children, Kenny was raised in a poor district of Houston. But his uncles were musicians, and Kenny formed his first band as a Jefferson Davis High School senior. He performed as a singer and an instrumentalist on guitar, bass guitar, piano, and harmonica. By 1966 he was a member of the famous New Christy Minstrels, but a year later, Kenny and other members of the Minstrels formed the First Edition, which soon would become Kenny Rogers and the First Edition.

The First Edition's initial hit came in 1968, "Ruby Don't Take Your Love to Town." In 1976 "Lucille" was an award-winning number one hit.

Two years later, Kenny had a run of five consecutive number one hits. Soon he began a series of duet recordings with female singers, most notably with Dottie West and Dolly Parton. In December 1984, the television special *Kenny and Dolly: A Christmas to Remember* was the highest-rated television program of the week. Kenny would continue to enjoy success with other TV specials. In 1991 Kenny's new duet partner was Linda Davis from Carthage, and they scored a hit with "If You Want to Find Love."

Tommie Ritter Smith had met Kenny backstage at the *Grand Ole Opry* and found him most congenial. Linda Davis put Tommie in touch with Kenny's people, and Linda was a smiling presence during his performance on the TCM-HOF stage.

Through the years, Kenny has received such stellar awards as Top Male Vocalist (multiple times), Top Vocal Duet (with Dottie West, with Dolly Parton, and with Ronnie Milsap), Single of the Year (multiple times), and Album of the Year (multiple times). In addition, in 2012, he released his autobiography, *Luck or Something Like It: A Memoir*.

But it is not luck that raised Kenny Rogers to such heights. In 2016 he launched *The Gambler's Last Deal*, a farewell tour in which he was accompanied on stage by Linda Davis. In addition, the Texas Country Music Hall of Fame was honored to host the renowned Kenny Rogers in one of his farewell appearances.

Kenny's TCMHOF appearance was part of his farewell tour, *The Gambler's Last Deal*. Lovely Linda Davis accompanied Rogers throughout this extended final schedule.

Unfortunately, health problems soon forced Kenny to cancel the remainder of his farewell tour. By 2020 he was under hospice care at his home. Kenny Rogers died of natural causes at the age of eighty-one.

* * * *

Bobbie Lee Nelson was asked about her *Audiobiography* by her famous brother, Willie. Bobbie planned, recorded, and released her *Audiobiography* CD in 2008. She explained to Willie why she titled it her *Audiobiography*;

"That is the way I could best express my autobiography," she said thoughtfully. "The story of our lives would be best told through music."

Bobbie was born on the first day of 1931 in Abbott, Texas. Abbott, in Hill County, was a cotton farming town of just over 200 people at that time. Two years later, Willie was born, but today, he always calls Bobbie his "little sister."

Soon their parents split and went separate ways, so Bobbie and Willie were raised in Abbott by their Nelson grandparents.

Grandfather Nelson was a blacksmith, but he shared a love for music with his wife. Grand-

Bobbie Lee Nelson from Abbott is a gifted pianist who frequently has accompanied her younger brother, Willie Nelson. Bobbie was inducted into the TCMHOF in 2017. She is shown with T.G. Sheppard, Linda Davis, and Kelly Lang.

mother Nelson had a small pump organ, and the couple sang and played and tried to write songs each evening. Her grandmother taught her chords on the organ when Bobbie showed an affinity for the keyboard. Grandfather Nelson saw that Bobbie had talent, and he bought a piano for $35. By age six, Bobbie could read music and learned to play.

Her first musical influence was gospel hymns at the Methodist Church in Abbott. The family attended a "sing" held in the ornate court house in nearby Hillsboro, and they heard the Stamps Quartet each Sunday morning on the radio. The radio also brought into the Nelson home the country sounds of the *Grand Ole Opry*, the *Louisiana Hayride*, the Light Crust Doughboys, and Bob Wills.

Bobbie became captivated by boogie woogie, but her grandmother hated this honky tonk music. "That was my first rebellion," laughed Bobbie, "to learn to play boogie woogie."

Bobbie and Willie performed together at churches and Abbott High School events as youngsters. Bobbie married at sixteen, and she and Willie played in a band organized by her husband. But the marriage broke up, and Bobbie was separated from her three sons for a time. Later, with custody of her sons restored, Bobbie worked in a Hammond Organ Company store in Fort Worth.

"It was the first time I had access to a music library," Bobbie recalled, and her musical horizons expanded. She played at restaurants to promote Hammond organs.

But with her sons grown, she rejoined Willie in the 1970s, first playing the piano for recording sessions, then joining a touring band — The Family. With Willie Nelson and The Family, Bobbie has entertained impressively for decades. She carries a seven-foot Steinway on the tour bus, and another favorite piano is at Willie's recording studio in Austin, where she lives.

Unfortunately, Bobbie's performance piano could not be delivered on time to Carthage, but even though she did not perform, she was a gracious presence onstage. "Little Sister" remains an exciting pianist with exceptional gifts. "I don't think Willie and I either one would be very healthy if we didn't tour," she explained. "It keeps us young and healthy and happy."

Sadly, Bobbie's health failed as she reached her nineties. She died in Austin on March 10, 2022, at the age of 91.

T.G. Sheppard and his wife, Kelly Lang were guest performers in 2017.

T.G. Sheppard up-close and personal with the TCMHOF audience.

Tracy Pitcox (left) of Brady, president of the Heart of Texas Country Music Association, was inducted into the TCMHOF Disc Jockey Hall of Fame in 2017.

Tracy Byrd of Vidor and Beaumont was a crowd-pleasing inductee in 2015.

The Oaks performing on the TCMHOF stage.

Award-winning DJ Dallas Wayne was inducted into the disc jockey wing of the Hall of Fame, and twice he has returned to the TCMHOF to emcee induction ceremonies.

Bobbie Lee Nelson with Dallas Wayne during her 2017 induction into the Texas Country Music Hall of Fame. Unfortunately, Bobbie passed away in March 2022.

Chapter Eight

The TCMHOF Enters Its Third Decade

Since its beginning, the Texas Country Music Hall of Fame has staged a full weekend of activities built around the Saturday evening induction ceremony and performance. In addition, of course, the museum and the gift shop are open to visitors on Fridays and Saturdays. A "Pickin' Party" entertained crowds with amateur talent at the local Esquire Theater on the first few Friday evenings. Throughout the day on Saturdays, amateur acts performed in the TCMHOF community room, which seats 300 while still affording space along the walls for vendor tables. Many stars signed CDs or books at these tables, while outdoor tables provided food.

In 2005 the Friday evening event evolved into the "John Ritter Tribute Showcase." With the enthusiastic support of the Ritter family, contestants sing and play, providing excellent country entertainment for modest admission costs. The contest winner is presented $1,000 and performs during the Saturday night induction show while functioning throughout the year as TCMHOF Ambassador.

On Saturdays on induction weekend, visitors are free to come and go to the museum and gift shop from 8 a.m. until 4 p.m.. From 9 a.m. until 1 p.m., Carthage radio station KGAS hosts the "Tex Ritter Roundup" of amateur entertainment, featuring a "Showdown Competition" at 10 a.m.. Meanwhile, "Downtown Country Music" begins at 2 p.m. at the Esquire Theater.

The feature event, of course, is the induction ceremony, held on Saturday evenings and occasionally lasting until midnight. Then, on Sunday mornings at 9 a.m. at the TCMHOF building, "Gospel at the Hall" is held, a religious service featuring performers — singers, instrumentalists, quartets — who are adept at southern gospel music. Gospel in the hall is the most appropriate, often inspiring, and emotional way to conclude a weekend devoted to Texas country music.

* * * *

In 2018, when the Chuck Wagon Gang was inducted into the TCMHOF, the gospel group eagerly participated in "Gospel at the Hall." Once a year, for an hour or two, the assembled attendees at the "Gospel in the Hall" experience the deep spiritual roots of Texas country music.

Among the unabashed admirers of the Chuck Wagon Gang was bluegrass star Marty Stuart, who was elated that the superb gospel group would be inducted into the TCMHOF in 2018. "This group was designed for the ages," stated Stuart. "For the eternal ages."

"Singing Chuck Wagon Gang music, there's nothing to hide behind, and nothing to lean on," declares Shayne Smith, the current owner, manager, and alto singer — and a granddaughter of original alto Anna "Effie" Carter and longtime guitarist Howard Gordon. "It's bare-bones, just voices and guitar, and that creates that unique sound. It's like the hard beginnings they all came from. Raw and tough, and you have to put it all out there."

The original Chuck Wagon Gang began putting it all out there more than eighty years ago. And from the hard beginnings of the 1930s, the

Chuck Wagon Gang became the most popular country gospel group of all time.

D.P. "Dad" Carter was born in 1889 in Kentucky but soon moved to Texas with his family. At a singing school in Clay County, Texas, he met Carrie Brooks. They married in 1909 and raised a family of eight. Dad Carter worked as a railroad brakeman and as a cotton farmer.

In 1935, desperate for extra money, Dad persuaded the management of radio station KFYO in Lubbock to air a daily program brought by the Carter Quartet for the beginning salary of $12.50 per week.

Dad sang tenor, while daughters Anna and Rose sang soprano and alto. The four-part harmony was rounded out by the deep bass voice of oldest son Jim, who added guitar accompaniment. (Jim was born in 1910 in the little farm town of Tioga, Texas, where Gene Autry was born in 1907.)

By 1936 the Carter Quartet moved to Fort Worth, where they were sponsored by Bewley's Best Flour over WBAP radio. At first, singing more cowboy music than gospel songs, they became known as the Chuck Wagon Gang. But fan mail from rural listeners clamored for more gospel songs. So after the change to gospel music, Bewley Mills offered a free picture of the Gang to anyone sending in a coupon found in a flour bag, receiving more than 100,000 replies.

The Chuck Wagon Gang disbanded during World War II but returned to WBAP and Bewley Mills in 1948. The Gang recorded for Columbia Records for forty years, eventually selling more than thirty million songs in the USA and overseas. In addition, there were appearances at the *Grand Ole Opry*, New York's Carnegie Hall, and the Hollywood Bowl.

After heart difficulties, Dad Carter stopped performing in 1955, and Jim Carter retired. Dad intended to make a special appearance in 1963 but collapsed backstage and died. Anna's husband, Howard Gordon, played guitar until his death in 1967. Several replacements to the Gang have been Carter family members. After Anna and Rose retired, younger brother Roy Carter

The Chuck Wagon Gang was inducted into the TCMHOF in 2018, and on Sunday morning the celebrated gospel group enthusiastically participated in "Gospel at the Hall," the final event of each induction weekend.

ran the Gang for many years.

In 1986 Dad Carter was posthumously elected to the Gospel Music Association Hall of Fame. Two years later, country music fans voted the Chuck Wagon Gang the top country/gospel group in America. More than seventy albums of the Gang's gospel recordings have been issued. Truly the Chuck Wagon Gang is a group designed for the ages.

* * * *

Following the splendid entertainment, the Chuck Wagon Gang provided, the 2,000-strong audience at the new Carthage High School auditorium welcomed Leon Rausch back to the TC-MHOF stage. When Bob Wills was posthumously inducted into the Texas Country Music Hall of Fame in 2000, Leon led a reunion band of the Texas Playboys at Bob's induction.

Likewise, Leon was delighted in 2011 when the Texas State Legislature proclaimed western swing the "State Music of Texas." And he was just as pleased when he was selected for induction into the Texas Country Music Hall of Fame. Although Rausch had been placed on oxygen, the veteran trouper sang vigorously at his ceremony.

Born in 1927 in Missouri, Leon was the only child of a musical couple. He learned to play several instruments, and little Leon stood at the microphone at the front of the family trio.

"I was eat up with it," laughs Rausch. "I thought I was going to be Gene Autry."

He performed steadily as a youngster, but after high school, Leon joined the U.S. Navy during World War II. After the service, he married his longtime sweetheart, Vonda Lee. Leon and Vonda had two children and a marriage that thrived for nearly seven decades.

During the 1950s, Leon moved his family to Tulsa and made radio appearances with a band led by the younger brother of Bob Wills, John Lee Wills. In 1958 Bob hired Leon as a Texas Playboy. Musical tastes were changing, however, and after a few years, Leon moved back to Tulsa, while Bob Wills fell into poor health and disbanded the Texas Playboys.

But in 1965, Leon was asked to return to Fort Worth to serve as manager and singer of a new version of the Texas Playboys. Bob appeared when his health permitted, and in 1973 he gathered top musicians to record a farewell album, *For the Last Time*. Unfortunately, Bob suffered a stroke and died in 1976.

Meanwhile, Leon continued with the band, which was renamed the Texas Panthers, a play on Fort Worth's early nickname, "Panther City." Leon's long identity with Fort Worth inspired Mayor Kay Granger to proclaim October 5, 1993,

Leon Rausch, lead singer of the Texas Playboys, performed at the 2000 induction of Bob Wills. Rausch returned to sing at his own induction in 2018.

as "Leon Rausch Day."

In 1975 a new version of the Wills band was formed, The Original Texas Playboys, with Rausch on vocals. The Original Texas Playboys toured for more than a decade, recorded several albums, and garnered various awards. Through the years, Leon performed at such noted venues as the John F. Kennedy Center for the Performing Arts, *Austin City Limits*, and the Golden Nugget Casino.

Members of the Texas Playboys came to accompany Rausch.

"People in Nashville liked me and had some recordings they wanted me to do," recalled Leon. "I tried that, but I guess I'm not that unique. I was more or less vanilla. I was just a band singer and a pretty fair dance band singer."

Leon's modest assessment of his career overlooks the steady audience demands of nearly nine decades and the high regard of generations of fellow professionals for this gifted country singer. Leon passed away in Fort Worth in 2019 at the age of ninety-one.

* * * *

Also, in 2018, the first female member of the Disc Jockey Wall of Fame was inducted. Jennifer Herron's warm, friendly voice has been heard by audiences worldwide.

Jennifer's path was determined early on. She grew up on a quarter-horse ranch in South Texas surrounded by dance halls, rodeos, and the characters that legends are made of. Her love of people, music, and swapping stories led Jennifer to a broadcast journalism degree which, in turn, has led her to some impressive career achievements in radio and television, as well as publicity with high-profile celebrities and events.

You can find her on Saturday nights serving as host/announcer on *Ernest Tubb Midnight Jamboree*, the longest-running radio show in history. Also, she is a guest announcer on the *Grand Ole Opry*.

Jennifer summed up her achievements by saying, "I was raised in Texas, where we were taught to work hard, care about others, and to always put your full heart into anything you do."

The addition of Jennifer Herron to the TCMHOF Disc Jockey Wall of Fame brought the total of Hall of Fame DJs to fourteen. But a key member died earlier in the year, in January 2018. Tom Perryman enjoyed a legendary career behind country music microphones for seventy years and was a member of Nashville's Country Music Disc Jockey Hall of Fame. Tom radiated a commanding presence at every induction weekend of the TCMHOF.

"I can truly say that there will never be another Tom Perryman," said Tommie Ritter Smith. "Everyone knew him, and he knew everyone. When he entered the room, there was no doubt he had arrived. From the very beginning of our journey into the country music world over thirty years ago, he was one of our biggest promoters. He has been an invaluable asset to the Texas

Country Music Hall of Fame, and we miss him."

* * * *

The 2019 TCMHOF was headlined, for the first time in ten years, by three inductees: Rodney Crowell, Claude Gray, and Jeannie C. Riley. A couple of years before her induction, Jeannie and her husband made an unannounced tour of the Hall of Fame Museum. Tommie Ritter Smith asked, "Did anyone ever tell you you look like Jeannie C. Riley?"

"That would be because I am Jeannie C. Riley." The two ladies became instant friends. Jean-

Jeannie C. Riley from Anson vaulted to stardom in 1968 with "Harper Valley PTA," and she was inducted into the TCMHOF in 2019.

nie stayed for hours, and she returned in 2019 as an inductee.

Jeannie C. Riley exploded onto the music scene in 1968 with her dynamic recording of "Harper Valley P.T.A." Her vibrant rendition of a small-town soap opera resonated with audiences. As a result, "Harper Valley P.T.A." shot to number one on both the Country Music Association and *Billboard* pop charts.

Jeannie earned a Grammy Award for Best Female Country Performer and the CMA Award for Single of the Year. In addition, she was nominated for Best New Artist and for Record of the Year. With worldwide sales of more than 5.5 million copies, "Harper Valley P.T.A." was awarded a Gold Disc only four weeks after the song's release. Another Gold Disc came when the album of the same name sold more than one million copies.

In 1969 Jeannie C. Riley became the first female vocalist to host her own network television variety special, *Harper Valley USA*. The popular

Jennifer Herron, a native of LaVernia, Texas, and a graduate of Texas State University, now headquarters in Nashville, where she hosts *Cheyenne Country*, Studio 23 Nashville, and the historic *Ernest Tubb Midnight Jamboree*. In 2018 Jennifer became the first female disc jockey inducted into the Texas Country Music Hall of Fame.

Jerry Reed was co-host, and there were guest appearances by Mel Tillis and the songwriter of "Harper Valley P.T.A.," Tom T. Hall.

In 1978 the song became a movie, *Harper Valley P.T.A.* with the lovely Barbara Eden starring as Mrs. Johnson, the song's central character. Eden continued the role in a 1981-83 television series.

As suggested in the song, the beautiful Jeannie C. Riley, clad in a mini-skirt and go-go boots, was enormously popular as a touring artist. She appeared on TV with such stars as Dean Martin, Bing Crosby, Tom Jones, and Bette Davis, as well as on *Hee Haw* and *The Ed Sullivan Show*.

Other hits by Jeannie C. Riley included "The Girl Most Likely," "The Dark Side of Dallas," "Country Cool," and "Good Enough to Be Your Wife." During her career, she has received five Grammy Award nominations and four CMA Award nominations.

A native of Anson in West Texas, Jeannie Carolyn Stephenson was a majorette in high school and sang in local jamborees. She married Mickey Riley and had a daughter, Kim Michelle. A move to Nashville resulted in a secretarial job at Passkey Music. She also recorded demos on the side and made the happy connection with "Harper Valley P.T.A."

During the late 1970s, Jeannie became a born again Christian. She exchanged her mini-skirts for conservative gowns and began recording gospel music. When she performed "Return to Harper Valley," she liked to end the song with the admonition: "Love One Another — Don't Judge One Another."

Jeannie was immensely pleased by her induction into the Texas Country Music Hall of Fame and by the enthusiastic welcome of the crowd. Unfortunately, there was no show the following year because of COVID, but in 2021 Jeannie C. Riley returned to the TCMHOF and was seated front and center, where she exchanged greetings with the stars performing on stage.

Another 2019 inductee was Claude Gray of Henderson, who at six-five was often called "The Tall Texan."

* * * *

Another noted artist from 2019 was six-foot-five-inch Claude Gray, who became known during his career as "The Tall Texan." Born in Henderson, Texas, in 1932, Gray was an accomplished musician who earned fame as a talented guitar picker, songwriter, and country singer with a smooth baritone voice. Gray, along with such artists as Jim Reeves, Eddy Arnold, Chet Atkins, and Ray Price, helped to create the Nashville Sound and the Countrypolitan movement, which attracted pop-oriented singers to country music and broadened the appeal of country to wider audiences.

Gray began recording while in Henderson High School, but after school, he joined the U.S. Navy, serving during the Korean War, 1950-54. Following his discharge, Gray worked as a radio announcer in Kilgore, Texas, and as a disc jockey in Meridian, Miss., while playing area clubs.

In 1959 Gray made his first recording, "I'm Not Supposed," a song that made the *Cash Box* country chart. *Cash Box* named Gray its Most Promising Country Singer. In 1960 Gray and his two friends paid $100 for the "Family Bible" song by Willie Nelson. "Family Bible" reached the top ten on the country charts and remains one of Gray's most memorable recordings.

In 1961 "I'll Just Have a Cup of Coffee (Then I'll Go)" reached number four on the charts, followed by "My Ears Should Burn (When Fools Are Talked About)," which was written by Roger Miller and which reached number three.

Gray fronted a popular tour act, the Claude Gray Roadshow, performing throughout the United States and parts of Europe. A staple of Gray's act was his version of Neil Diamond's "Sweet Caroline." Gray has performed in Branson and is often introduced as "a man you have to look up to."

* * * *

Singer-songwriter-record producer Rodney Crowell came by his talent naturally. One of his grandfathers was a church choir leader, and the other was a bluegrass banjo picker, while a grandmother played guitar. In addition, Rodney's father was an active musician throughout his life.

Born in Crosby in 1950, Rodney later moved with his family to the Houston area. By the time he was eleven, Rodney played drums with his father's band. In 1965 Rodney organized his own band, the Arbitrators.

Rodney moved to Nashville in 1972 to pursue music as a full-time career. Soon he was discovered by Jerry Reed, who recognized his gifts and immediately boosted his activities in Nashville's musical world.

From that point on, Rodney Crowell has earned one success after another. He carefully studied the craft of songwriting, and his songs have been recorded and performed by such artists as Johnny Cash, Lynn Anderson, Waylon Jennings, Roseanne Cash, Alan Jackson, Bobby Bare, Crystal Gayle, Vince Gill, Lee Ann Womack, Kris Kristofferson, Emmylou Harris, the Oak Ridge Boys, the Nitty Gritty Dirt Band, and LaCosta (sister of Tanya Tucker). In addition, of course, Crowell recorded a number of his own songs.

In 2003 Rodney Crowell was inducted into the Nashville Songwriters Hall of Fame.

Also inducted in 2019 was singer-songwriter-record producer Rodney Crowell of Crosby and Houston.

the words of his 2017 Song of the Year, "It Ain't Over Yet."

* * * *

Planning for the 2020 ceremony began, and Tommie Ritter Smith secured contracts with quality performers. But as the year 2020 advanced, the COVID epidemic spread throughout the United States and the world. As a result, enormous changes occurred in American society, including the closure of museums and the cancellation of public events. Hopes that conditions soon would improve vanished and the Texas Country Music Hall of Fame was forced to cancel the induction weekend scheduled for August 2020.

The financial blow to the TCMHOF was serious because the annual induction celebration is the only substantial fundraiser for the Hall of Fame. But the TCMHOF had funds built up in reserve, and there were donations from local benefactors and admissions from museum tickets. As a result, the TCMHOF weathered the difficulties of 2020 and looked forward to 2021.

Sadly, COVID conditions continued into 2021, and it proved difficult to schedule potential inductees. It was decided to stage a concert, to put on a lively country music show that would entertain fans and raise money for the TCMHOF.

Moe Bandy agreed to perform, and so did Jeannie Seely and Janie Fricke. Linda Davis and Lang Scott were eager to help. T.G. Sheppard would be one of the "Special Guests" of 2021, along with lovely Mandy Barnett, a regular on the *Grand Ole Opry*. An appearance was made by U.S. Congressman Louie Gohmert, togged out in a Western hat and boots and jeans. Gohmert brought his guitar and several friends who helped him perform entertaining country music.

Dallas Wayne emceed the event, which was held at the Carthage Civic Center. A Pioneer Award — only the fifth ever issued — was presented to Tommie Ritter Smith to honor her

Popular Moe Bandy was a headliner of the 2021 show.

Three years later, he was awarded the Lifetime Achievement in Songwriting, and the following year he was inducted into the Music City Walk of Fame. Crowell twice won Grammy Awards, in 1990 for Best Country Song, "After All This Time," and in 2014 Best Americana Album for *Old Yellow Moon*. Twice, in 2013 and 2016, Rodney and Emmylou Harris were honored as Best Duo of the Year.

Rodney is the proud father of four daughters, three during his marriage to Roseanne Cash and one from a brief marriage early in his Nashville years. Since 1998 he has been wed to Claudia Church.

Rodney's album *Texas* was released at the same time as his TCMHOF induction and featured mostly other Texas artists. Rodney Crowell continues to be honored for his stellar career. In

husband, Bill. Bill Smith had aided Tommie throughout the history of the Tex Ritter Museum and the subsequent Texas Country Music Hall of Fame. But, Bill "Ritter" Smith developed health difficulties, and he died, at the age of seventy-seven, not long before the 2021 ceremony. The tribute to Bill was one of the most powerful moments of the evening.

Although attendance was down slightly in 2021, many tickets were paid for but not used, perhaps because of the COVID scare. Nevertheless, the 2021 celebration was a financial success, and as this book goes to print, plans are being shaped for a memorable 2022 event — which will be the twenty-fifth anniversary of the Texas Country Music Hall of Fame.

Guest performer Janie Fricke was a two-time winner of the CMA Female Vocalist of the Year Award.

Jeannie Seely, a TCMHOF veteran, was welcomed back in 2021.

Linda Davis and her husband, Lang Scott, also were guest performers in 2021.

Another 2021 guest performer was Mandy Barnett, a *Grand Ole Opry* regular.

Dallas Wayne, shown here with the lovely Linda Davis.

Congressman Louie Gohmert brought his guitar and several friends to the TCMHOF stage.

Appendix A
Hall of Fame Inductees

1998	Tex Ritter Gene Autry	Jim Reeves Cindy Walker	Willie Nelson Joe Allison
1999	Ernest Tubb Bill Mack	Waylon Jennings	Hank Thompson
2000	Bob Wills	Dale Evans	Charlie Walker
2001	Ray Price	Stuart Hamblin	Billy Walker
2002	Tanya Tucker	Gene Watson	Nat Stuckey
2003	Kris Kristofferson	Lefty Frizzell	Johnny Bush
2004	Mac Davis	Johnny Lee	The Big Bopper (J.P. Richardson)
2005	Roger Miller Johnny Gimble	Glenn Sutton	Jimmy Dean
2006	Larry, Steve, Rudy Gatlin	Billy Joe Shaver	
2007	Johnny Rodriguez	Red Steagall	Bob Luman
2008	Buck Owens	The Whites	Mickey Newbury
2009	Linda Davis	Neal McCoy	Michael Martin Murphy
2010	George Jones	Al Dexter	Ray Winkler
2011	Mickey Gilley	Moe Bandy	
2014	Duane Allen and the Oak Ridge Boys		
2015	Tracy Byrd		
2016	Clint Black		
2017	Kenny Rogers	Bobbie Nelson	
2018	Leon Rausch	The Chuck Wagon Gang	
2019	Jeannie C. Riley	Rodney Crowell	Claude Gray

Appendix B
The Disc Jockey Wall of Fame

Joe Allison	Doug Collins
Paul Kallinger	Bill Mack
Tom Perryman	Mike Oatman
Larry Scott	Pappy Dave
Smokey Stover	Charlie Walker
Joe Bielinski	Dallas Wayne
Tracy Pitcox	Jennifer Herron

Appendix C
Pioneer Awards

James Kirkland

Johnny High

Bill Smith

James White

Mo Jelaudarzadeh

Appendix D
Texas Country Music Hall of Fame
Original Executive Board of Directors

Tommie Ritter Smith	President
Chester Stout	Vice President
Charles Thomas	Secretary
Lynn C. Vincent	Treasurer
Warren T. Biggs	Assistant Treasurer

Appendix E
Tex Ritter Museum Original Executive Board of Directors

Tommie Ritter Smith	President
Charles Thomas	Vice President
Brenda Samford	Secretary
John Ritter	Director
Tom Ritter	Director

Appendix F

Tribute to Bill Smith

Bill Smith happily played a unique role in the life of the Texas Country Music Hall of Fame and the Tex Ritter Museum. Indeed, he often was called "Bill Ritter Smith", a nickname he responded to with a chuckle and a big smile.

William Everett "Bill" Smith was born in 1944 in Haynesville, La., and was a star athlete at Haynesville High School, and he was awarded a track and cross country scholarship to Northeast Louisiana University. Bill would continue distance running throughout most of his life, and he took pride that at the age of forty-three he qualified for and participated in the famous Boston Marathon.

As a young man, Bill served in the U.S. Air Force. Following his discharge his business career brought him to Carthage, Texas, where he managed one of the Ben Franklin franchises owned by his family. Later Bill was associated in Carthage with Panola Savings and Loan and with Complete Printing and Publishing. He was active in the Lions Club and the First Baptist Church.

But even more notable than his athletic achievements or his business abilities or his community involvement, Bill Smith deeply loved Southern gospel music.

Bill expressed his musical passion with a splendid bass voice, focusing his talents on Southern gospel songs. In 1983 Bill joined a popular new gospel group, the Calvary Boys. The Calvary Boys were based in Tenaha, less than 20 miles from Carthage. The addition of a gifted bass singer added an important element to the Calvary Boys. The singers were constantly on the road, performing at churches and various events across the South. The Calvary Boys recorded in Nashville and were in great demand for concerts.

A highlight of a Calvary Boys performance was "Give the World a Smile Each Day," the gospel classic that was the theme song of the famed Stamps Quartet. "Give the World a Smile" features a striking bass part, always performed with remarkable style and enthusiasm by Bill Smith.

In 1994 Bill married the director of the Panola County Chamber of Commerce, Tommie Ritter Smith. She also founded the Tex Ritter Museum, and soon she created the Texas Country Music Hall of Fame. Bill "Ritter" Smith aided Tommie at every step with these major projects. No task was too large, and Bill Smith was an instrumental figure in the amazing growth of the Texas Country Music Hall of Fame.

Of particular note was his performance, usually for tourist groups, as Tex Ritter. Bill would dress in one of Ritter's Western suits, along with a pair of cowboy boots and a cowboy hat. Bill Ritter Smith then would deliver Tex Ritter songs in a rich, deep, crowd-pleasing voice. Bill passed away in March 2021, and he is profoundly missed.

Index

About the Authors

Tommie Ritter Smith, like Tex Ritter, Jim Reeves, and Linda Davis, is a native of Panola County. Tommie grew up in a musical family, and as a young lady, she visited the Reo Palm Isle, Billy Bob's Texas, Gilley's, and other important country music venues throughout Texas. For nearly three decades, Tommie has dreamed and worked to create a museum in her hometown that would honor the country musicians of Texas. Traveling from Nashville to Branson to Hollywood and points in between, Tommie became personally acquainted with a significant number of country artists and executives. Since 1998 Tommie has organized major concerts at the Texas Country Music Hall of Fame, and she has collected a massive amount of memorabilia for display at the TCMHOF.

Bill O'Neal is the award-winning author of more than fifty books, including biographies of Tex Ritter and the Sons of the Pioneers. In addition, bill has appeared in television documentaries on CMT, History Channel, A&E, Learning Channel, TBS, and American Heroes Channel. Following Bill's appointment by Governor Rick Perry as State Historian of Texas, he has traveled tens of thousands of miles across the Lone Star State as an ambassador for Texas history and culture. Bill enjoyed a long career on the history faculty at Panola College in Carthage, and in 2013 Panola's new dormitory was named Bill O'Neal Hall. That same year, he received an honorary Doctor of Letters Degree from his alma mater, Texas A&M University-Commerce.

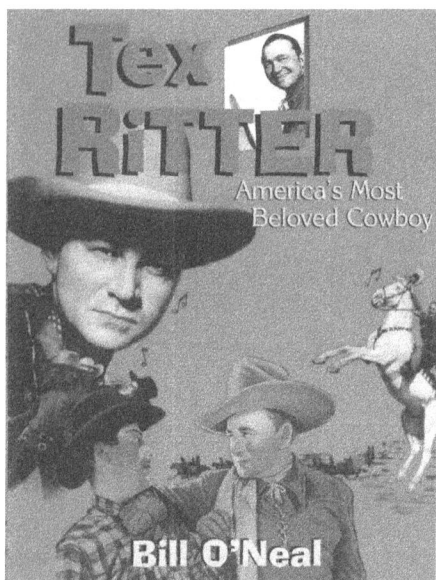

www.ingramcontent.com/pod-product-compliance
Lightning Source LLC
Chambersburg PA
CBHW081426090426

42740CB00017B/3194